The Souldrop Cookbook

Compiled by Kay Bone

Proceeds to ADDISS
Supporting children and adults with ADHD
Attention Deficit Hyperactivity Disorder

The *Souldrop* *Cookbook*

Compiled by Kay Bone

Published by

ADDiSS
ADHD INFORMATION SERVICES

Published in the UK in November 2009 by

ADD Information Service Ltd
2nd Floor, Premier House
112 Station Road
Edgware
Middlesex HA8 7BJ
Email: info@addiss.co.uk
www.addiss.co.uk

ISBN 978 0 955 4033 47

Cover design and typesetting by braden-threadgold.com
Printed and bound in the UK by Alpine Press

Sean Anthony Bone
25.08.1987 – 12.09.2008

Smile and be happy when you remember me

Old Church Farm 1924.

All Saints Church, Souldrop.

The Bedford Arms, Souldrop.

Fundraising day at Souldrop
Village Hall

Contents

Foreword

This book is dedicated to my son Sean, who lived in the village of Souldrop in Bedfordshire and had ADHD. Sadly, he took his own life in 2008. He had overcome many of the life challenges of ADHD but, in the end, he felt that he could not cope anymore. He died a very popular, sensitive and funny young man, much loved by all his friends and family. All proceeds of this book will go to ADDISS for their ongoing work, as it is very dear to my heart.

The Souldrop Cookbook is a fundraising effort for ADDISS, the national Attention Deficit Hyperactivity Disorder Information and Support Service. They provide information, training and support for parents, sufferers and professionals in the fields of Attention Deficit Hyperactivity Disorder (ADHD). It is a registered charity (1070827)

ADHD is a developmental disorder related to the frontal lobe of the brain. It is very common, affecting 3-5% of children, with a high proportion carrying symptoms into adulthood. The disorder is recognised as one of the most important causes of problems that children have with school work, and relationships with friends and family. These problems often have long term consequences so that about two thirds of children with ADHD have persistent problems which affect them as adults. By investigating the causes and finding out how genes and environments can combine to bring about ADHD, we will be in a far better position to develop the best and most effective approaches to help individuals with ADHD.

Thank you to everyone in Souldrop who has kindly donated recipes, photographs, and helped to proof read and write up some of the recipes and made this book possible. Special thanks to Jeremy Viewing for sharing his vast knowledge of our village's history, and to everyone who buys this book, raising awareness of ADHD and funds for ADDISS. Also, not forgetting Nancy Mills of Souldrop, who donated quite a few recipes in this book, which I collected, sadly just after she passed away. I hope people really enjoy cooking these, as I thought what a wonderful cook Nancy must have been, as I wrote them up!

Thanks also to Paul (Sean's Dad and best friend), and Clare Bone (Sean's sister) for their patience, help and encouragement in compiling the Souldrop recipe cookbook.

And very special thanks to my son Sean, who I was privileged to have and to know as my son for 21 years, for giving me the inspiration to compile this book.

I hope a greater understanding of ADHD through Sean's life will be achieved as people become more aware of this often misunderstood disorder.

Kay Bone.
Mother of Sean Bone

Souldrop

SOULDROP is one of the most northerly villages in Bedfordshire. It is situated off the A6 and is reached by a minor road, known as Stocking Lane. The winding nature of the lane, appears to look like a stocking laying on the ground. There is an alternative route into the village, via Sharnbrook, which is again a pretty road to travel, past a beauty spot known for generations as Bluebell Bank.

The name Souldrop has been derived from various spellings from early times, one being Southdrope, as the land slopes away to the south of the village.

The village is made up of about seventy odd dwellings with some dating back to the 16th century. Lamb's Cottage (left) is of particular interest, being partly built of daub and wattle, before being burnt down in 1965, when it had a thatched roof.

Old articles about the village mention a manor which is thought to be somewhere between Church Farm and Middle Farm. There were four farms in the village, Town, Church, Middle and Cross Weir farm (only two working), but no remaining thatched cottages. The village hall was previously a school, which was built in 1861 at the time of the rebuilding of the church. The children in Souldrop now attend schools in Riseley or Sharnbrook.

The public house is known as The Beds Arms and is still a popular meeting place. It was

originally partly built of stone with daub and wattle but suffered a serious fire in 1969. It was replaced by a brick building but many of the old features have been retained.

In 1924, Mr Spavins was the landlord of the Bedford Arms and purchased the three listed cottages, next door to the pub. The cottages were previously used to house the farm workers. These 18th century cottages were originally owned by the  Colworth Estate, and were sold for £880 each, to Mr Spavins. They were made of limestone rubble with a pantile roof and are now Grade 2 listed.

The body of the village church was made of wood but this was burnt down in the early 19th century. The church was rebuilt in 1863/1864 by the Duke of Bedford but the 13th century bell tower is all that remains of the original church.

 A dispute arose in the 14th century over the living of the church. There was a disturbance which started at the church gates, and continued throughout the churchyard to the church. The rector and his followers managed to lock themselves up in the church, and got up into the bell tower, pulling up the ladder behind them. The rivals tried but failed to burn down the church, and then a fight began with bows and arrows. The rector's supporters had an

Souldrop (cont.)

advantage over the rivals, due to their high position in the bell tower. A man was killed, and his wife attempted to bring an action against the rector, but there was no evidence to determine who fired the fatal arrow.

There was originally a village pump at the entrance to Church Farm, where the village people fetched their water from for many years. This disappeared when the main water supply was added in the early 20th century. Villagers then fetched their water from the lion hydrants which were placed down the roadside verges. The village pound also disappeared when it was developed in the late 1950's, and the land was used to build Souldrop's only community housing.

There was no electric power in Souldrop until 1962. At that time, the majority of houses still had no running water and used oil lamps.

Forty Foot lane was used by drovers as part of the way to take animals on route to St Neots and other markets.

The railway from London to the North, was built during 1857/1860, and passed through part of a parish. The men who worked on the buildings of the up and down lines were housed in a 'shanty town' of huts. Two men were killed during these operations and were buried in the churchyard. Iron memorials mark their graves.

There was originally a sub post office operating at the 'Old Post Office', which is now a residential property. This moved to the school house in the early 1960's for the convenience of the villagers, but is no longer used for that purpose. There is also no shop in Souldrop now, and residents must travel to Sharnbrook, Rushden or Bedford.

Souldrop's achievement is not to have become a suburb of Rushden or Sharnbrook, as is sadly the case of Wymington. The Castaways Club on the A6 was originally the Sharnbrook Road House, which was said to be the first American Diner built outside the USA.

In thirty years, the village has increased by 50%, but the main street is a no through road. Souldrop therefore remains a quiet backwater enjoyed by many people who care to take time and wander through and admire the architecture and different buildings, which are found in this beautiful village.

The Souldrop Cookbook

Enlarged map of Souldrop Village 1924 (Bedfordshire and Luton Archive Centre).

Souldrop High Street with Mrs Ritch standing by the wall 1910 (copy of an early 20th century postcard).

Looking back down Souldrop High Street, September 2009.

Souldrop High Street 1924, with Lambs Cottage on the right, with the original thatched roof.

Lamb's Cottage.

The three Grade 2 listed cottages (built 1750), that were originally used to house the farm workers.

Part of a building belonging to Bedford Arms – where doves and bats live.

An autumnal day, looking over the front view of the Old Church Farm, where sheep graze and the baby lambs are born in the spring.

All Saints Church, Souldrop.

Old Church Farm House – The Gullivers sold the land and outbuildings to Nigel and Monica Russell, but continued to live in the house. It is now separate to the working farm (Church Farm).

Oven Temperature Conversion Chart & Abbreviations

	°F	°C	Gas Mark
Very cool	225	110	1/4
	250	120	1/2
Cool	275	140	1
	300	150	2
Moderate	325	160	3
	350	180	4
Moderately Hot	375	190	5
	400	200	6
Hot	425	220	7
	450	230	8
Very Hot	475	240	9

G – Grams

Mls – millilitres

L – Litres

Oz – ounces

Dsp – dessert spoon

Tsp – teaspoon

Tbsp – tablespoon

Souldrop Starters

Butternut Squash Soup

1 medium sized butternut squash
1 large onion
2 medium sized carrots
Salt and cracked black pepper
1 tbsp oil
2 pints water
3 medium potatoes
Vegetable stock granules

- Peel butternut squash, cut in half, remove seeds and cut into chunks.
- Peel onion, carrots and potatoes and cut into chunks.
- Heat oil in pan and cook onions until soft. Add water, stock, butternut, carrots, potatoes, salt and pepper.
- Cook until soft, then remove from heat.
- Put in a blender, and blend until smooth. Add a little water, if too thick.
- Serve with crusty bread. Serves 4-6.

Recipe donated by Daphne Papworth, Souldrop

Souldrop Starters

Creamy Red Pepper and Butternut Squash Soup

1oz butter
½ pt milk
1 large onion
Salt and pepper
1 medium butternut squash, deseeded and cut into chunks
1 red pepper, deseeded and chopped
2 vegetable stock cubes, dissolved in 1 pint of hot water

- Melt butter in large saucepan.
- Add onion and fry gently for 3 minutes, until soft but not brown.
- Add butternut squash, red pepper and vegetable stock.
- Heat until simmering, then turn heat to low and cook for 20 minutes, partially covered until soft and tender.
- Transfer to blender. Blend 15-20 seconds until smooth.
- Return to pan, add milk and seasoning.

Recipe donated by Julie Wallinger, Souldrop

Curried Parsnip Soup

2oz butter
1 medium onion skinned and sliced
2lb parsnips, peeled and finely diced
1.25 tsp curry powder
0.5 tsp cumin
3 pts vegetable stock
Salt and pepper
Single cream **(5 fl oz)**

- Heat the butter in the base of a large pan and fry the onion and parsnips for about three minutes.
- Stir in the curry powder and cumin, and then fry for a further two minutes.
- Add stock, bring to the boil, reduce heat, cover and simmer for 45 minutes until vegetables are tender.
- Cool slightly then blend the vegetables.
- Return to the pan, add salt, pepper & cream, reheat to serving temperature but do not boil.

Recipe donated by Amy Maddison, Souldrop

Souldrop Starters

Leek and Potato Soup

2 lb potatoes, peeled and diced
4 leeks, sliced and washed
2 onions, chopped
2 pints vegetable stock
Mixed herbs
Salt and pepper
Cream (optional)

- Lightly fry the onion.
- Add leeks, potatoes and stock and bring to the boil.
- Simmer for 15-20 minutes or until potatoes start to break up.
- Add the salt and pepper and mixed herbs to taste.
- Blend and serve with a drizzle of cream.

Recipe donated by Sally from the Bedford Arms Pub in Souldrop

Speedy Sweet Potato Soup with Coconut

1 tbsp. vegetable oil
1 onion – chopped
1-2 tsp Thai curry paste (red or green)
750 gms/1 lb 10oz sweet potatoes, grated
1 ltr/1 ¾ pints vegetable stock
½ sachet creamed coconut (or use ¼ can coconut milk)
Handful coriander, roughly chopped
Mini naan bread to serve

- Preparation time – 10 minutes.
- Cooking time – 10 minutes.
- Heat the oil in a deep saucepan, and then soften the onion for 4-5 minutes. Stir in the curry paste and cook for 1 min more. Add the grated sweet potato and stock, and then bring quickly to the boil, simmering for 5 minutes until the sweet potato is tender.
- Remove the soup from the heat, stir in the coconut and seasoning, then cool briefly before whizzing with a stick blender (or in a food processor) until smooth. Season to taste. Sprinkle with chopped coriander and serve with warm naan breads. Serves four.

Recipe donated by Kim Kelly, Souldrop

Souldrop Starters

Sweet Potato, Apple and Ginger Soup

1 onion chopped
Parsley
1 tbsp flour
Thyme
1 large sweet potato or **2** small, peeled and chopped
Bread croutons
1 large cooking apple or 2 sweet ones
Milk
Piece of root ginger grated, **about 1tbsp**
Chicken stock cube in **1 pint** of boiling water

- Fry onion in a large saucepan. Add flour.
- Stir in, and then add boiling water and stock cube.
- Add chopped sweet potatoes, apple and ginger. Simmer for 45 minutes.
- Stir in some milk and thicken with a little cornflour if liked.
- When cooked, either strain through a sieve or put in food processor to blend.
- Add salt and pepper to taste.
- Serve in warm bowls with toasted croutons, spread with olive oil and sprinkle on parsley and thyme.

Recipe donated by Nancy Mills, Souldrop

Aubergine Parcels

A variation on the mozzarella and tomato thyme for a starter.
Ingredients are approximate.

2 large long aubergines
225/8oz mozzarella cheese
2 plum tomatoes
16 large basil leaves
2 tbsp olive oil
Salt and ground black pepper
2 tbsp toasted pine nuts
Extra basil leaves to garnish

Dressing
4 tbsp extra virgin olive oil
1 tsp balsamic vinegar
1 tbsp sun-dried tomato paste or puree
1 tbsp lemon juice

- Remove the stalks from the aubergines and cut the aubergines lengthways into thin slices – try to get an even number as you need two per parcel.
- Bring a large saucepan of salted water to the boil add the aubergine slices and cook for approximately 2 minutes until just softened.
- Drain the aubergines and dry them on kitchen paper
- Cut the mozzarella into eight slices, then cut the tomatoes into eight thin slices (discard the end slices).
- Take two aubergine slices and place on a tray or dish in a cross. Place a slice of tomato in the centre season with salt and pepper then add a basil leaf followed by a slice of mozzarella another basil leaf a final slice of tomato and a little more seasoning.
- Fold the ends of the aubergine slices around the mozzarella and tomato filling to make a neat parcel
- Repeat with the rest of the filling until you have used all the ingredients (makes approximately eight parcels).
- Chill the parcels for 20 minutes.

To make the dressing

- Whisk together the olive oil, vinegar, sun-dried tomato paste and the lemon juice – Season to taste.
- Pre-heat the grill.
- Brush the parcels with olive oil and cook them for about 5 minutes on each side until golden.
- Serve hot with the dressing sprinkled with toasted pine nuts and basil leaves.

Recipe donated by Mari and Joe Zafar, Souldrop

Souldrop Starters

FungHi Arrabiati

700g button mushrooms
2 dry chillies
1 tin of chopped tomatoes
Fresh basil

3 tbsp oil
Mozzarella cheese
2 cloves garlic
Salt to taste

- Fry mushrooms with crushed garlic and chilli for five minutes.
- Add tomatoes and basil and cook for 10 minutes.
- Divide into four oven proof dishes and top with mozzarella cheese.
- Bake for 5-10 minutes at 200 C until lightly brown. Serves four.

Recipe by Silvana Sharpe, Souldrop

Tuna Dip

1 tin tuna – drained
1 tsp lemon juice
5 tbsp mayo

¼ tsp Worcester sauce
1 tbsp tomato ketchup

- Mix altogether and serve with crisps or vegetable sticks and breadsticks.

Recipe donated by Jann Horton, Souldrop.

Melon Creation

2 galia melons
1 red grapefruit
2 tbsp of grapefruit juice (from the grapefruit)
Small piece of ginger, peeled and grated **(about 2cm)**
2 tbsp of clear honey
200g of large prawns
Lettuce
Paprika

- Cut the melons in half, scoop out the seeds and throw them away.
- With a sharp knife cut all the melon out so you are left with a thin bowl.
- Cut the melon you have scooped out into cubes and place in a large bowl.
- Turn the melon shells upside down and leave to drain.
- Scoop out the grapefruit and cut into cubes, add to the melon.
- Add the prawns to the melon and grapefruit.
- In a small bowl, mix together the ginger, honey and grapefruit juice.
- Add the dressing to the melon, grapefruit and prawns, stir and leave to stand.
- To serve, place lettuce in the bottom of each of the melon shells and top with the melon mixture.
- Spoon over any remaining dressing and sprinkle over some paprika.

Recipe donated Kristy Mead, Souldrop

Cecil Gulliver at the Souldrop Fete in 1974 .
Cecil Gulliver was a weatherman and farmer.
After the weathercock fell off the church
steeple in a storm, Cecil put a copy of it on his
hat as he was the 'village weather'. He had a
column in the Anglia News and liked to wear
his hat on high days and holidays.

Old Church Farm 1924.

Church Farm, October 2009.

Looking from the field behind
Church Farm and All Saints Church,
Souldrop. October 2009.

Old Church Farm.

Side view of Church Farm taken from
Gullivers Spinney with All Saints Church
Souldrop on the left, October 2009.

Black Pepper Prawns

2 tbsp dark soy sauce
2 tbsp Chinese cooking wine
2 tbsp oyster sauce
1½ tsp sugar
2 tbsp black peppercorns
4 tbsp butter
1 medium red chilli, sliced

4 coin-sized slices of fresh ginger
4 big cloves of garlic, finely chopped
About 20 curry leave, fresh or dried (optional)
800g raw big prawns

- Mix together the soy sauce, wine, oyster sauce and sugar.
- Coarsely grind the peppercorns in a pestle and mortar (or buy coarse ground black pepper!). Throw them into a dry wok and toast for a minute over a low heat. Tip out and keep to one side.
- Wipe out the wok, melt the butter and add the chilli, ginger, garlic and curry leaves. Stir for a minute to soften.
- Throw in the prawns and stir-fry until they start to turn pink, then sprinkle in the ground pepper and stir in well.
- Add the sauce and bubble until thick and syrupy. Add 1-2 tbsp of water and cook again until the sauce is thick enough to coat the prawns.
- Serve with noodles or rice. Serves two.

Also good with strips of chicken!

Recipe donated by Mandy Sharland, Souldrop

Broccoli and Salmon Bake

250g penne pasta
8 sun dried tomatoes,
drained and thickly sliced
300g broccoli florets
2 tbsp capers
25g butter
8 anchovy fillets, halved

25g plain flour
10 fresh basil leaves
600mls milk
4 skinless salmon fillets
100g mascarpone
50g mature cheddar, grated.

- Preheat oven to Gas Mark 5
- Boil a large pan of salted water, add pasta, and then boil for 6 minutes.
- Add broccoli to pasta and cook for 4 minutes. Drain well.
- Put the butter, flour and milk in a pan and heat, stirring continually until it thickens to a smooth sauce. Remove from heat and add mascarpone, tomatoes, capers, anchovies and basil.
- Add the pasta and broccoli to the sauce. Season well.
- Halve the salmon fillets and place the pieces in a single layer on the base of an ovenproof dish.
- Spoon the broccoli mixture on top, then scatter with the cheddar.
- Bake for 30 minutes until the mixture is just starting to bubble round the edges and the mixture is pale golden.

Recipe donated by Donna, Souldrop

Souldrop Fish Dishes

Chermoula Tuna Skewers

This is a fantastic recipe that I came over by chance after arranging a barbeque for some friends. I had bought some cubed fresh tuna, but had not thought more about what to do with it. I searched the net for ages and then took a chance as most the ingredients exist in every household. The skewers were a success and I have now provided many friends with the recipe that has been adored by everyone who has tried or heard about it. It is quick to produce and only requires two hours of marinating. The dish originates from Morocco.

1 ¼ lb fresh tuna	**1 tsp** course salt
1 tsp cumin	Freshly ground pepper
1 tsp paprika	**½ bunch** chopped coriander leaves
1 tsp turmeric	
¼ tsp cayenne pepper	**½ bunch** chopped parsley
2 garlic cloves minced	**½ lemon** squeezed to juice
1 medium onion coarsely grated	**3 tbsps** extra virgin oil

- Cut the tuna into 1 inch cubes.
- With a mortar and pestle, or in a blender or food processor, mix together the cumin, paprika, turmeric, cayenne, garlic, onion, salt, pepper, coriander, parsley, lemon juice, olive oil and 1 tablespoon of water. Pour over the tuna and mix well. Leave to marinate for 2 hours.
- Heat the griddle pan, grill or barbecue.
- Divide the tuna into 12 parts and thread the tuna onto the skewers. Set the tuna skewers on a platter until ready to grill. Reserve the marinade.
- Grill the tuna skewers over a medium-hot barbecue or grill for 5 to 8 minutes, turning every few minutes and brushing occasionally with the marinade. Remove from the heat and place on the platter. Garnish with lemon wedges and serve immediately.

Recipe donated by Nina and Mick Chivers, Souldrop

Kedgeree

½ **cup** of rice
½ **cup** frozen peas
2 hard boiled eggs
1oz butter
1 piece of haddock or white fish
Salt, cayenne pepper and curry powder
1 chopped onion

- Boil rice until cooked, and then drain.
- Boil fish, and then flake it.
- Lightly fry the onion and cook the peas.
- Chop up the eggs.
- Add fish, onions, peas and eggs to the rice.
- Add salt, cayenne pepper and curry powder.
- Melt butter in a pan or microwave and cook everything under gentle heat until thoroughly hot. Stir occasionally.
- Serve hot.

Recipe provided by Robert Freeman, Souldrop

Paella

4 chicken breasts	**1** bottle white wine
100g frozen peas	**5mls** of turmeric
400g of paella rice	**1** chicken stock cube
Small bunch of flat-leaf parsley	Sea salt & ground pepper
220g large prawns	**100g** chorizo sausage
1 onion	**2** lemons
20 mussels	**4** rashers of smoky streaked bacon
2 cloves garlic	
1 piece white fish	Freshly grated parmesan
5mls hot paprika	**100g** of green beans

- Scrub the mussels – steam fish & slice into small pieces.
- Chop the parsley leaves and stalks.
- Cut the chicken into bite-size pieces – slice up the chorizo into 1cm squares and slice the bacon.
- Chop the garlic and onion.
- Make the stock (about 1/3 of a pint).

Cooking the paella

- Put a good drizzle of olive oil in a large paella pan/ wok.
- Add the parsley, chicken, chorizo, bacon and cook for about 5 minutes.
- Add the onion and garlic and cook for a little longer.
- Add the paella rice, paprika and turmeric to the pan with a good pinch of salt and pepper and stir for one minute.
- Pour in half a bottle of wine and hot chicken stock and bring to the boil, stir frequently. Put a lid on the pan and turn down the heat to simmer, cook rice according to the packet instructions (You may need to add a little more wine as it cooks – test the rice by tasting).
- Whilst there is still some liquid, pour over the peas and beans.
- Stir in the sea food and squeeze over the juice of one lemon.
- Cook for a further 10 minutes, making sure the mussels are open and the prawns are pink.
- Serve with some lemon wedges and some freshly grated parmesan cheese to sprinkle over the top.

Recipe donated by Kristy Mead, Souldrop

Poached Haddock with Mussels, Spinach and Chervil

150g/5oz butter
1 shallot, finely chopped
600mls/1pint mussels, cleaned
4 x 175g/6oz pieces of unskinned haddock fillet
900g/2lb fresh spinach, washed, large stalks removed

1 tbsp malt whisky
1 tsp fresh lemon juice
1 tsp chopped chervil
salt and freshly ground black pepper

- Heat 1oz of the butter in a medium pan, add the shallot and cook gently for three minutes, until soft. Add the mussels and 5fl oz of water, then cover and cook over a high heat for 3-4 minutes, until the mussels have opened. Tip them into a colander set over a bowl to collect the cooking liquor. When they are cool enough to handle, remove the mussels from all but 8 of the nicest shells. Cover and set aside.

- Pour all the mussel liquor except the last tablespoon or two (which will be gritty) into a 12in sauté pan, bring to a simmer and then add the haddock, skin-side up. Cover and simmer gently for 3 minutes. Remove from the heat (leaving the lid in place) and set aside for about 4 minutes to continue cooking.

- Meanwhile, melt another 25g/1oz of the butter in a large pan. Add the spinach and stir over a high heat until it has wilted. Cook, stirring briskly, until all the excess liquid has evaporated, then season to taste with some salt and pepper.

- Divide the spinach between 4 warmed plates and put the haddock on top. Keep warm. Return the sauté pan to the heat, add the remaining butter and boil rapidly for 3-4 minutes, until the liquor has reduced and emulsified into a sauce. Stir in the whisky and lemon juice and boil for 30 seconds. Add the chervil and mussels and stir for a few seconds, until they have heated through.

- Spoon the mussels around the spinach and haddock, dividing the unshelled mussels equally between the plates, then pour over the sauce and serve. Serves four.

- Serve with warm crusty bread to mop up the juices!

Recipe donated by Jon Smith, Souldrop

33

Souldrop Fish Dishes

Smoked Salmon & Prawn Pasta

Mug of king prawns
Slice of smoked salmon
Mug of peas
A few asparagus spears

Shallots or red onions
Any pasta - I like spaghetti
Butter
Seasoning and single cream

- Cook pasta al dente and place to one side
- Gently fry the sliced onion in butter
- Then add peas, asparagus, prawns and salmon until all cooked lightly
- Season well add pasta a few spoons of single cream
- Serve with hot crusty bread or salad.

You can make this a little more adventurous by adding some white wine when you first add all the ingredients. It's down to personal choice...

Recipe donated by Julie Grout, Souldrop

Tagliatelle al Salmon e Vodka

500g of fresh green tagliatelle
¼ chopped onion
200g smoked salmon
50ch or double shot of vodka,

2 tbsp chopped parsley
250mls of double cream
or Elmlea double cream
50g butter

- Sauté onions lightly in butter.
- Add strips of salmon and sauté quickly.
- Add vodka and stir for a few minutes.
- Add cream, parsley and fresh black pepper. Cook for a few minutes.
- Cook tagliatelle, add to the sauce and stir.
- Serve on a platter and sprinkle with parsley. Serves four.

Recipe donated by Silvana Sharpe, Souldrop

Spaghettini with Prawns

Bag of raw tiger prawns

6 – 8 cherry tomatoes

1 clove of garlic, crushed

Spaghettini or linguine

¼ tsp chilli (I use the crushed-in-oil type from a jar, but dried flakes are acceptable)

2-3 tbsp extra virgin olive oil

2 – 3 tbsp finely chopped flat leaf parsley

- In a large frying pan, lightly sauté the garlic and chilli in the extra virgin oil.
- Add the chopped parsley and stir it around adding the halved cherry tomatoes. Squash these with your fingers as you add them, to release their juice.
- Cook gently for 5-10 minutes.
- Add the raw tiger prawns (cut them in half lengthways, if they are really big), cooking until they turn pink.
- Boil the pasta until al dente.
- Drain and toss it into the frying pan with the prawns.
- Mix together and serve.

A great 'girlfriend' lunch dish, but also loved by my husband. It must be his Italian roots.

Recipe donated by Caroline Rich, Souldrop

Old Church Farm, October 2009.

The Gullivers at the Old Church Farm plucking shed, which still remains.

Reg Gulliver plucking turkeys at the Old Church Farm. This is now a residential property but Church Farm (built in 2002) still supplies turkeys.

Old Church Farm.

Monica Russell, the farmer's wife, holding one of their pet turkeys.

Church Farm, October 2009.

Church Farm (built in 2002), on the original grounds of the Old Church Farm, which was sold with the outbuildings to Nigel and Monica Russell in 1996.

Old Church Farm turkeys.

Souldrop's hog roast – annual event for villagers and their friends and families, on the village green. July 2009.

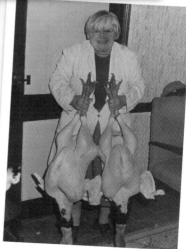

Miriam Gulliver, with turkeys at the Old Church Farm.

Bedfordshire Clanger

For the filling
1lb minced meat (beef or lamb)
1 onion finely chopped
1oz butter
Salt and pepper to taste
2 large apples, cleaned, cored and diced
1 oz raisins or blackberries
2 tbsp sugar

For the suet pastry
Suet
8oz flour
½ tsp salt
1 tsp baking powder
cold water

- For the suet pastry - mix suet, flour, salt, baking powder.
- Add cold water to form a light elastic dough which leaves the bowl clean.
- Roll out the pastry into an oblong and cut off from each of the short sides.
- Place the pastry off-cuts in the middle of the oblong to make a divider.
- For the filling - In a large frying pan melt the butter and fry meat and onions.
- Season to taste, and when golden brown remove and allow to stand.
- In one half of the pastry put the meat mixture and in the other half place the fruit, along with the sugar.
- Damp edges and roll up – mark the meat end with an X so you know where to start eating.
- Place in a floured bag and tie up.
- Place in a saucepan and cover with boiling water and cook for 1 ½ hours.

Recipe donated by Jeremy Viewing, Souldrop

Bedfordshire Roll & Sauce

For the filling	For the suet pastry	For the sauce
2 onions	**3-4 oz** suet	**4** onions
¼ lb minced meat	**8oz** flour	**1** stick celery
2 rashers of streaky bacon	**½ tsp** salt	**1** carrot
Salt & black pepper	**1 tsp** baking powder	Parsley stalks
1 oz flour	Cold water	Seasoning
¾ pint stock		
1 oz dripping		

- For the suet pastry - mix suet, flour, salt and baking powder together.
- Add cold water to form a light elastic dough which leaves the mixing bowl clean.
- For the filling - Par-boil the onions and chop roughly.
- Mince the meat and bacon.
- Roll the suet pastry into an oblong.
- Spread with onions and meat and season with salt and black pepper.
- Damp edges, roll up and tie in a floured cloth.
- Boil for 2 hours.
- To make the sauce - peel the onions and place in a saucepan with celery, carrot and parsley.
- Season with salt and pepper, and cover with stock (Oxo or meat stock).
- Cook until onions are tender. Allow to cool then strain off the liquid into a bowl.
- Remove onions and chop finely.
- Make a roux by melting the dripping, add the flour and fry until brown.
- Add the stock by degrees and boil.
- Replace the chopped onions and season, allow stock to thicken.
- To serve, remove the cloth from the roll and turn onto a hot dish, pour the sauce over the roll.

The suet roll is a traditional Bedfordshire recipe, using left over Sunday meat. This is a "hard calorie" meal for railway & factory workers, regarded as stodgy nowadays!

Recipe donated by Jeremy and Tina Viewing, Souldrop

Beef & Tomato Cobbler

For the filling	2 tbsp English mustard
1 oz margarine	1 tsp black pepper
1 onion (copped)	
4 oz mushrooms (chopped)	For the topping
3 tbsp plain flour	8 oz self raising flour
1 beef stock cube	½ tsp salt
1lb minced beef	2 oz margarine
1 tin chopped tomatoes	¼ pint milk
1 tbsp tomato puree	3 oz grated cheese
1 tsp mixed herbs	1 egg (beaten)

- Melt the fat and gently fry the onion until soft. Add the mushrooms and sauté for 2 minutes. Sprinkle in the flour and mix well. Crumble in the stock cube and stir in the remaining filling ingredients. Bring to the boil and then simmer for 10 minutes, stirring occasionally.
- Prepare the topping; Sift the flour and salt, and then rub in the margarine to fine breadcrumbs. Mix to a soft dough with the milk and then knead on a floured surface.
- Roll to an oblong 15x7 inches and sprinkle with the grated cheese, salt and pepper.
- Roll up lengthways and then cut into 12 rounds.
- Pour the beef mixture into a large oven-proof dish and then arrange the scones overlapping on the top. Brush with egg or milk and bake at 200°C for about 30 minutes until the topping is golden. Serves 4.

Recipe donated by Jenny Briggs, Souldrop. Jenny's mother gave it to her.

Beef Stew & Dumplings

½ **lb** beef steak
9 oxo cubes or 3 pints stock
1 onion
8 oz flour
2 carrots
1 tsp baking powder

1 stalk celery
4 oz suet (Atora)
3 large mushrooms
Salt and pepper
1 clove garlic

Beef stew

- Cube beef and put into a bag with the flour. Shake until well covered.
- Heat the pan with oil/butter and fry a finely chopped onion.
- Place beef and onion into a four pint stew pot and add 2 pints of stock.
- Slice the carrot, celery, garlic and mushrooms, and add to the beef and onion.
- Place in a preheated oven at 180° and cook for 1 ½ hours.
- Remove from the oven, stir and add the remaining stock. Cook for another hour.
- Remove and add the dumplings, cook for 40 minutes longer.

Dumplings

- Mix 8oz flour with 4oz suet, 1 tsp salt and 1tsp baking powder.
- Add water until mixture is stiff and all flour is absorbed.
- Leave to stand for ½ hour.
- Roll out on a floured table into a sausage. Divide and roll into several sections.
- Roll into balls.

This recipe was traditionally used with poor cuts of meat, so the garlic was used to lift the flavour of the meat.

Recipe donated by Jeremy Viewing, Souldrop

Souldrop Meat Dishes

Braised Lamb with Cannellini Beans

2 tins of cannellini beans
250g tinned tomatoes
1 leg of lamb, cut into chunks
2 dried chillies
A couple of handfuls of flour
5 tbsp crème fraiche
Pinch of ground cumin

1 celeriac
1 tbsp ground coriander seeds
chopped thyme
3 tbsp olive oil
salt and pepper
2 bay leaves

- Preheat oven to Gas 5.
- Cut lamb into large squares and dust with the flour mixed with the ground spices.
- Heat some oil in a large pan and brown the lamb until dark, then remove and place in an ovenproof dish.
- Stir in the bay leaves, tomatoes, beans and chillies and season. Now add half a pint of water (or lamb stock) and dot in the crème fraiche.
- Peel the celeriac and chop into cubes. Mix it with some olive oil, seasoning and thyme, and then add it to the lamb.
- Cook in the oven for 2 hours, removing the lid for the last ½ an hour.

Recipe donated by Donna, Souldrop

Bonfire Night Chicken

8 chicken thighs
or **4** chicken legs

1 level tbsp white sugar

1 large clove garlic, peeled,
crushed and finely chopped

1 tbsp red wine vinegar

4 rounded tbsp tomato ketchup

½ tsp Worcestershire sauce

3 tbsp soy sauce

1 level tsp ground cumin

3 tbsp vegetable oil

½ level tsp hot chilli powder

½ level tsp dried
mustard powder

Sea salt & ground pepper

- First make the marinade. Combine all the ingredients, except the chicken in a bowl, and whisk them together thoroughly.
- Make a few diagonal slashes through the chicken skin and flesh.
- Put the chicken into a dish and pour the marinade over the top.
- Leave for at least 4-8 hours.
- Then take the chicken out of the marinade and place them, skin side down in a roasting dish.
- Put the chicken in the oven and cook for about 50 minutes, turning the chicken half way through.
- Baste the chicken at this stage.
- The chicken should be well cooked, with a dark brown, sticky-crispy glaze.
- Serve immediately with a lot of paper napkins and spicy roast potatoes. (see page 81). Serves 4.

Recipe donated by Caroline Rich, Souldrop

Chang Mai Curry (Jungle curry)

2 tbsp yellow bean sauce

1 tbsp chopped lemon grass

2 tbsp red curry paste

1 tbsp fresh root ginger

4 green chilli peppers
(De- seeded)

dash of shrimp paste (optional)

2 tbsp caster sugar

60mls lime juice

4 cloves garlic chopped

500mls coconut milk

3 shallots, chopped

450g braising steak,
cut into strips (or chicken,
fish or vegetables)

- Place yellow bean sauce, red curry paste, chillies, sugar, garlic, shallots, lemon grass, ginger, shrimp paste and lime juice in a blender and blend to a paste.
- Put beef (or chicken/fish/vegetables) in a casserole with coconut milk. Bring to the boil, cover and simmer gently for 45 minutes or until tender.
- Add blended ingredients and cook for a further 10 minutes.
- Serve with Thai rice and naan bread.

Recipe donated by Karen Johnson, Souldrop

Charlie's Chicken Curry

This is a delicious healthy meal that looks and sounds more complicated than it is. I love cooking this and it tastes absolutely stunning. It's even better with a nice bottle of rose wine.

25g butter
1tsp ground/ fresh ginger
1 diced onion
400g tin of chopped tomatoes
4 chicken breasts
2 x 200mls cartons of coconut cream
1 chopped red chilli
large handful of coriander leaves

- Melt butter in a large frying pan and add diced onion and chilli.
- Fry onion until soft but not brown then add the chicken breasts and seal both sides.
- Then add the tin of tomatoes, all the coconut cream and ginger.
- Stir then cover and simmer for about 25 minutes (stirring occasionally).
- Bosh the coriander in for flavour.
- Serve with rice. Serves 4.

Recipe donated by Charlie Butler-Henderson, Souldrop

Souldrop Meat Dishes

Chicken in Mayonnaise

Chopped cooked chicken

Diced pineapple

6 dsp mayonnaise

2 dsp natural yoghurt

1 dsp tomato ketchup

1 tsp Curry powder

A sprinkle of garlic powder

- Combine all the ingredients and mix well.
- Serve with salad or jacket potato.

Recipe donated by Jenny Briggs, Souldrop. Jenny's mother gave it to her.

Home Made Beef Burgers

1lb lean steak mince

salt

1lb pork mince

1 egg

Cracked black pepper

1 medium onion, chopped finely

- Mix steak mince and pork finely together.
- Add onion, salt and pepper.
- Mix well.
- Lastly, add the egg.
- Shape in burger mould if you have one, if not use an egg ring.
- Cook under medium grill for about 7 minutes each side or as desired. Makes 20-24.

Recipe donated by Daphne Papworth, Souldrop

Kay's Chicken & Cashew Nuts, with Sweet and Sour Sauce

Chicken
2 Chicken breasts
Cashew nuts
Red pepper
Onion
Garlic
Salt and pepper
Ginger
4 mushrooms
Dried chillies

Tin of Chinese vegetables / bamboo shoots / beansprouts / water chestnuts

Sweet and Sour Sauce
1/3 cup of rice vinegar
4 tbsp brown sugar
1 tbsp tomato ketchup
2 tsp cornflour
4 tsp water
1 tsp soy sauce

- Heat Chinese oil in a wok and fry cashew nuts until browned. Remove.
- Cut chicken breasts into pieces and fry until cooked. Remove.
- Cut all vegetables into chunks and fry in Chinese oil, over a high heat until browned. Remove.
- Make sweet and sour sauce. Mix corn-flour in water. In a saucepan, add vinegar, brown sugar, tomato ketchup and soy sauce and bring to the boil. Add corn-flour mixture to thicken. Keep on low heat.
- Return chicken, nuts and vegetables to the wok and heat, add salt, pepper and ginger, then pour over sweet and sour sauce.
- Serve with Kay's egg fried rice. (see page 77)

Kay's tip – I always buy my chicken from Brown's butchers at Stagsden. It is succulent and moist. Try it and taste the difference!

Recipe donated by Kay Bone, Souldrop

Souldrop Meat Dishes

Chicken Stir Fry with Cashew Nuts

1 cup chicken stock

1 medium stalk broccoli, cut into small florets

1 tbsp cornstarch

1 medium onion, chopped into ¼ rings

2 tbsp soya sauce

1 red pepper, cut into 1" pieces

½ tsp sesame oil

2 or 3 chicken breasts, (depending on size), cut into pieces

1/2 - 2/3 roasted cashew nuts

1 cup of cooked rice

1 – 2 tbsp cooking oil

- Mix chicken stock, cornstarch and soy sauce together and set aside.
- Cook chicken in wok, and then remove with juice into a spare dish.
- Put vegetables with a ¼ cup of stock mixture into wok. Let cook until crispy and crunchy.
- Add in the rest of the mixture, and chicken, along with juices.
- Cook for 2 – 3 minutes or until boiling. Boil for one minute.
- Remove from heat and add in cashew nuts and sesame oil. Stir and serve over rice.

Recipe donated by Sheila and Ken's niece, Abi Graves, Souldrop

Chicken Valdastana

4 chicken breasts
Mixed herbs
½ pt double cream
2 slices ham, cut in half
Cracked black pepper and salt
Drizzle of oil
4oz cheese

- Butterfly – cut open and spread out - the chicken breasts and put on baking tray.
- Sprinkle with mixed herbs, salt and pepper.
- Drizzle with oil and place in medium oven 180° for 30 minutes.
- Remove from oven.
- Put half a slice of ham on each chicken breast and a handful of cheese.
- Then pour the cream over and return to the oven for a further 30 minutes until golden brown and bubbly.
- Serve with mash and veg or chips and peas.

Recipe donated by Daphne Papworth, Souldrop

Souldrop Meat Dishes

Chilli Con Carne

8oz dried red kidney beans (in Chilli sauce)	**1tbsp** flour
1tsp paprika	**2** garlic cloves crushed
4tbsp oil	salt
1tbsp tomato puree	**1kg/2lb** minced beef
2 onions chopped	**2x14 oz cans** tomatoes.
	1-2 tbsp chilli powder

- Heat oil in pan. Add onions and garlic and fry until golden.
- Add beef and fry for 5-6 minutes, stirring constantly.
- Stir in chilli powder, paprika, tomato puree, flour and salt to taste, and cook for 2 minutes.
- Add tomatoes and beans, mix thoroughly and bring to the boil. Lower heat, cover and simmer for 1-1 ½ hrs, stirring occasionally. Taste and adjust seasoning.
- Serve with rice and garlic bread.

Variation of recipe without the rice

- Line a casserole dish with a layer of chilli hot Doritos, then a layer of chilli mixture (as above).
- Spoon a layer of crème fraiche over, then another layer of Doritos.
- And finally a layer of grated cheese.
- Grill under oven till golden brown and serve.
- Serve with garlic bread. If feeling very brave, can serve with additional fresh red chillies in olive oil.

Beware of mornings though!

Kay's tip – I either buy my beef locally for this at Hurley's farm shop in Sharnbrook or Brown's Farm Shop at Stagsden. Both do excellent meat.

Recipe donated by Kay Bone, Souldrop
(Sean's mum – this was Sean's favourite recipe)

Easy Spaghetti Bolognaise

500g minced beef

1 level dessert spoon
herbes de province

1 large onion

1 medium red bell pepper

½ tin carrots (420g approx)

1 level tbsp sugar/canderal

2 tins chopped tomatoes
(400g approx)

1 tbsp tomato puree

3 cloves of garlic

- Brown meat in olive oil.
- Then add finely chopped onion, bell pepper
  (having removed seeds and pith).
- When soft, add crushed garlic to taste.
- Stir for one minute, and then add all other
  ingredients, retaining some tomato juice,
  if the mixture becomes dry.
- Simmer for 5 minutes.
- Then pour into casserole and cook in microwave
  on defrost for 30 minutes. Serve with spaghetti.

Recipe donated by Marie Keating, Souldrop

James' Cottage Pie

450g beef mince	Flour
6 rashers smoked streaky bacon roughly chopped	**250mls** quality beef stock
1 medium onion	Salt and Pepper to season
100g vacuum packed chestnuts	Olive oil
	Mashed potato to cover

- Pre-heat the oven to 180C.
- Chop the onion very finely while heating 3-4 tps of oil in a heavy non-stick frying pan over a medium to low heat. When the oil is hot, fry the onions for around 5 minutes or until they are quite soft and starting to brown.
- Remove the onion and fry the bacon until it starts to colour. Add the fried onion a few turns of salt and pepper, crumble in the mince and the chestnuts.
- Once the mince is browned all over, remove any excess water from the pan. If you use good mince from the farm shop or butchers this won't happen.
- Add 2-3 dessert spoons of flour or enough to soak up any fat in the pan. Cook for 30 seconds.
- Add the stock slowly mixing it in until you have a thick gravy covering the meat - don't let it get to runny.
- Cook for 1 minute and check for seasoning.
- Place in an oven proof dish and cover with a good smooth buttery mashed potato. Fork over the top to give some texture.
- Place in the oven for 25-30 minutes or until the top is golden.
- Serve with steamed fresh veg and HP sauce.

Recipe donated by James Rogers, Souldrop

James' Creamy Curry

2 good sized chicken breasts, chopped in to 3 cm pieces

1 large onion

Enough oil to cover the bottom of your pan completely

3 cloves

5 peppercorns

½ **tsp** fennel

½ **tsp** cumin

½ **jar** Patak's madras curry paste, for a medium curry

9 **dsp** plain yoghurt

1 chopped fresh chilli

200mls double cream

Handful of sliced almonds

2 **cups** of rice

- Heat the oil in a heavy bottomed pan over a medium heat. When hot add the chicken and fry it till it starts to colour. Remove the chicken and place to one side.
- Finely chop the onion. Add the onion and the spices to the oil you fried the chicken in and fry until soft and lightly browned.
- Add the Patak's paste - and fry it for 1-2 minutes.
- Now add the yoghurt. This needs to be done very slowly. Turn the heat down to low and add 2-3 spoons at a time letting each lot start to bubble a little before the next one. Go too quick and it curdles like mad.
- Add the chicken and the chopped chilli.
- Give it a good stir and then add the cream.
- Cover and let it simmer for at least 40 minutes.
- As the curry cooks the oil will rise to the top and you can carefully spoon it off.
- Wash the rice in several changes of water until it the no longer makes the water cloudy. Drain it well.
- Place the rice and 3 cups of boiling water and a good pinch of salt in a microwave proof dish with a lid.
- Blast in the microwave till it boils. Then microwave for around 8 minutes on the lowest setting you have. Check to see that all the water has been absorbed and the rice is fluffy and light. If not give it more time.
- To serve heat a dry frying pan over a medium to low heat - be careful as you can damage your non stick if you get it too hot, place the almond slices in the pan and toast them for a few minutes.
- Load the rice on a plate, add the curry and the almonds and eat.

Recipe donated by James Rogers, Souldrop

Souldrop Meat Dishes

Jenny's Five Hour Lamb

1 leg of lamb
Sprigs of rosemary
2 cloves garlic, cut into small slithers
Roasting bag or foil

- Make small cuts in the skin of the lamb about 2" apart and insert a small sprig of rosemary or small slither of garlic alternately into the cuts. Do this all round the leg.
- Put the lamb into a roasting bag or wrapping foil.
- Place in a deep roasting tin and cook for about 5 hours at gas mark 2/130°C/300°F.
- Turn or baste after 2 hours. It may be necessary to reduce the time for smaller joints.
- When cooked, the meat should be soft, succulent and shrunk slightly from the bone.
- Serve with a rich lamb gravy made to your own favourite recipe or with a good quality stock cube.

This dish is best complimented by Greek roast potatoes (see page 77) **and mixed roast vegetables.** (see page 79) **Enjoy!**

To complete the Greek experience, follow this with a Baklava, a sweet honey and nut desert. (see page 92)

Recipe donated by Jenny Deacon, Souldrop

Lancashire Hotpot

1lb diced lamb
2 leeks, sliced and washed
2 onions, chopped
1 small swede, peeled and diced
1 pint beef stock
Mixed herbs, salt and pepper
1 lb potatoes, peeled and sliced thinly
4 oz butter

- Place lamb, leeks, onions, swede, stock, salt and pepper and herbs in a pan.
- Bring to the boil and simmer until meat is tender.
- Place meat mixture in a deep dish and lay sliced potatoes on top.
- Put knobs of butter on potatoes and sprinkle with salt and cracked black pepper.
- Place in the oven on gas mark 6 for 20-30 minutes until potatoes are cooked.

Recipe donated by Sally,
The Bedford Arms Pub, Souldrop.

Lasagna

Meat sauce ingredients	
450g (1lb) minced beef	Pinch dried oregano
55g (2 oz) streaky bacon	Oil for frying
2 medium onions, chopped	**White sauce and cheese**
2 sticks of celery, chopped	**45g (1 ½ oz)** butter
55g (2 oz) mushrooms sliced	**45g (1 ½ oz)** flour
15g (½ oz) plain flour	**5mls (1 level tsp)** mustard
200mls (8fl oz) beef stock	Pinch nutmeg
50mls (2fl oz) red wine	**500mls (1pt)** milk
85g (3 oz) tomato puree	Salt & ground black pepper
1 Clove of garlic, crushed	**195g (7 oz)** cheddar cheese, grated
Salt & ground black pepper	**110g (4 oz)** uncooked lasagna

- Fry the mince until browned and broken up. Drain and set aside. Fry the bacon. Drain and place with the mince.
- Fry the onions and celery for about 5 minutes, add the mushrooms and return to the mince and bacon, stir in the flour cook for 1 minute.
- Add the stock and wine and stir until boiling, add remaining meat sauce ingredients. Stir well and simmer, covered for 1 hour.
- Make white sauce. Melt butter, stir in flour, mustard, and nutmeg and seasoning, cook gently for 2 minutes.
- Remove pan from heat, stir in milk and bring back to the boil. Stir until thickened and smooth.
- In a casserole, place a third of the meat sauce, a third of the white sauce and a third of the cheese, followed by half of the uncooked lasagna. Follow this with another third of the meat sauce, white sauce and cheese and the rest of the lasagna. Finish by layering the rest of the sauces and cheese on top.
- Leave the lasagna to go completely cold.
- Bake at 160 °C (Gas mark 3) for 45 minutes until the top is golden brown. Serves 6.

Recipe donated by Julie and Bob Hancock, Souldrop

Grandad Mills' Macaroni Cheese with Bacon

2 oz butter	Rashers of bacon
tsp Mustard	**¼ lb** cheese
1 dsp flour	Dash of Worcester sauce
Paprika pepper	Macaroni
½ cup milk	Parmesan cheese

- Melt the butter, add flour and brown it.
- Add mustard, Worcester sauce and milk. Thicken.
- Then add cheese.
- Cook macaroni in milk, then mix with sauce.
- Put in ovenproof dish.
- Sprinkle with parmesan cheese and paprika pepper over the top.
- Put rashers of bacon over.
- Grill till brown under the grill then turn the bacon over.
- Serve immediately.

This recipe was my Dad's and Sean loved it! My Dad would cook it for Sean when he went up to visit his Grandad in Ravensden. Any cooking skills I inherited are attributed to my Dad. I used to so love his cooking. God bless you, Dad. (I don't think he will have any time for cooking in heaven now, as he will be busy chasing Sean around!)

Recipe donated by Kay Bone, Souldrop

Souldrop Meat Dishes

Meat Loaf

1lb minced beef
3 tbsp milk
1lb pork
1 ½ tsp mustard powder
2 medium onions, finely chopped
2 tbsp Worcester sauce
3 cloves garlic, peeled
4fl oz dry white wine

4 tbsp chopped fresh parsley
8 slices smoked streaky bacon
1 tbsp chopped fresh thyme
salt & black pepper to taste
1 large egg
3oz white bread, sliced and crusts removed, cut into 1" cubes

- Chop the onions, garlic, parsley and thyme altogether.
- Add the meats, and break in the egg.
- Place the bread in a large bowl, spoon in the milk.
- Mix with hands until all broken into small crumbs, add everything together, finely chopped and mixed.
- When the mixture is ready, pack into 2lb loaf tin (7 ½" x 4 ¾" x 3 ½" deep). Smooth off the top.
- Lay the bacon on top, slightly overlapping.
- Cover with foil and twist the corners.
- Stand tin in shallow baking tin. Pour in about an inch of boiling water.
- Place in middle of oven.
- Cook slowly for about 2 hours.
- After that remove foil and pierce the meat loaf with a skewer, press down to make sure the juices are running clear.
- Let it cool for about 30 minutes. If serving cold, replace foil and weigh down until completely cold.

Recipe donated by Karl Haska, Souldrop

Norfolk Meat Patty

Short crust pastry
4oz plain flour
4oz Self Raising flour
2oz lard
2oz margerine
Salt
1 egg (beaten)
Water

Filling
Small onion
1lb minced beef steak
1 tsp mixed herbs
2 tsp Worcester or HP sauce
15fl oz water
salt & pepper

- Fry chopped onion in a little oil or lard, for a few minutes to soften.
- Stir in mince and brown it all over.
- Stir in about a tablespoonful of flour.
- Pour on boiling water and turn down to simmer.
- Add sauce, herbs, salt and pepper.
- Put lid on and cook for 20 -25minutes.
- Cool. Reserve some liquid (used for gravy).
- Make pastry – rub fat in flour or blend in processor.
- Add salt, half the egg and 3 tbsp water to form a stiff paste.
- Leave to chill in fridge for 15minutes.
- Roll out in 2 circles.
- Line a greased 7" tin or deep pie dish with one half of pastry.
- Put in mince, top with other half of pastry, seal edges, trim off extra round dish.
- Brush with other half of egg.
- Make a hole in the top.
- Bake in hot oven 200° for 10 minutes then turn down to 180° for another 20 minutes until browned.
- Make gravy with left over liquid, extra water and thicken with Bisto. Serve with fresh vegetables.

Recipe donated by Nancy Mills, Souldrop

Oven Baked Chicken with English Apples

You can use any cut of chicken for this recipe. It's a nice summer dish using fresh cooking apples.

Approximately 8oz of chicken per person
½ **tsp** salt
¼ **tsp** black pepper
½ **tsp** sage
Small splash olive oil
1 chicken stock cube

250mls apple juice
250mls boiling water
2 large cooking apples peeled and diced
1 **tbsp** cornflour
1 **tsp** cinnamon

- Sprinkle both sides of chicken with salt and pepper. Place chicken in shallow frying pan with a little olive oil to stop sticking and brown off until all sides completely seared.

- Remove from pan and place chicken in casserole dish. Dissolve stock cube in boiling water. Pour over chicken along with apple juice. Add sage. Cover and bake for 25minutes in a 180 c. degree oven or until almost cooked.

- Mix cornflour with a little cold water and pour over chicken and stir. Add apples and cinnamon. Bake uncovered for 10 minutes until apples are just soft and fluffy around the edges but with some crispness.

- Serve with fresh carrots, broccoli and buttered new potatoes. Serves four.

Recipe donated by Beth Ring, Souldrop

Pork a la Creme

1 ½ lb pork fillet	salt & pepper
1 beef stock cube	**1 level tbsp** paprika pepper
2 tbsp oil	**6 oz** butter mushrooms
5 tbsp sherry	**1 level tbsp** plain flour
1 oz butter	**1 level tbsp** cornflour
1 level tsp tomato puree	**½ pt** water
1 onion, peeled and chopped	**5oz carton** double cream

- Cut pork into 1 ½ inch cubes.
- Heat oil and butter in pan, then fry pork pieces quickly until just turning brown. Remove and drain on kitchen paper.
- Fry onion and paprika, blend in flour. Cook for 1 minute. Remove from heat.
- Blend in stock. Add sherry, tomato puree and return to heat.
- Simmer until thick. Season with salt and pepper.
- Add the meat.
- Cover and simmer 30 – 40 minutes until tender.
- Then add mushrooms.
- Blend cornflour to paste with cold water (2 tbsp) and add to pan.
- Reheat and add cream.
- This can be decorated with triangles of fried bread and sprigs of parsley.
- Serve with potatoes and peas or sweet corn.

Recipe donated by Nancy Mills, Souldrop

Souldrop Meat Dishes

Satay

Not for peanut allergy sufferers.

Marinade for 1lb meat
fillet of lamb is best
4 small chopped red onions
2 cloves garlic
3 stalks of serai (lemon grass)
1 tsp cumin
1 tsp ginger powder (or some chopped up root ginger)
1 tbsp turmeric
1/2 tsp ground black pepper
1/2 tsp of salt
1/2 tsp of sugar
2oz (50mls.) light soy sauce

Sauce
6 small red onions
3 cloves of garlic
3 stalks of serai (lemon grass)
1 tsp chilli powder
1 cinnamon stick
2 tbsp sugar
salt to taste
1oz (25mls.) lime juice
4oz. (100gm.) ground peanuts
2oz. (20 mls.) coconut milk
2oz. (50 mls.) oil
6oz. (150 mls.) water

- Marinade the meat for at least an hour.
- Cut meat into small cubes. Chop onions, garlic and serai and pound together with other ingredients.
- Mix in the spices and then mix thoroughly with the meat and allow to stand for at least an hour.
- To make the sauce chop the onions, garlic and serai and stir fry in a little oil for 5 minutes. Add all the other ingredients and bring to the boil. Then simmer for 15 to 20 minutes.
- Place meat onto skewers and cook over charcoal turning and basting with oil frequently.
- If no barbeque, put in the bottom of a grill pan with a bit of oil and remember to keep turning!
- Serve the meat and sauce with raw onion and wedges of cucumber. I usually serve it with rice as well.

This is my favourite recipe which was passed on to me by a Malaysian friend called Ooi Peng Hooi way back in the 70s.

Recipe donated by Susan, Souldrop

Sausage and Apple Plait

1 chopped small onion
1 **tsp** ground thyme
1 **tbsp** of oil
salt and pepper
2 sticks of celery, diced
1 egg, beaten

1 small apple, peeled and chopped
½ **tsp** mild curry powder
1 **lb** good quality sausage meat
8oz puff pastry

- Fry the onion until soft.
- Add the celery, apple, sausage meat, thyme, seasoning, half the egg and curry powder.
- Allow to cool.
- Roll the pastry out into a rectangle and spread the mixture down the centre of the pastry.
- Brush the remaining edges of the pastry with beaten egg and make a series of diagonal cuts at quarter inch intervals down the longest sides of the rectangle.
- Starting at one end, fold the strips over, overlapping in the centre to form a plait.
- Continue until the filling is completely covered.
- Paint the plaited top with beaten egg.

- Bake in a preheated oven at 220°C for 15 minutes.
- After this time, reduce the heat and cook for a further 20 minutes until the pastry is crisp and golden.
- Serve hot or cold with braised red cabbage and a baked potato. Serves 4 -5 people.

This keeps well in a freezer and is ideal for a quick lunch or picnic and is good with spicy chutney.

Recipe donated by no 14, Souldrop

Souldrop Meat Dishes

Sausage, Apple & Herb Pie

8oz short crust pastry
freshly ground pepper
12oz pork sausage meat
1 egg
4oz bacon
3 tbsp freshly chopped parsley
1 cooking apple

- Roll out pastry and line 8" flan dish with half the pastry.
- Fork together sausage meat, chopped bacon, grated apple and add beaten egg.
- Stir in herbs and pepper.
- Fill flan dish. Top with rest of pastry. Brush with beaten egg.
- Bake 10 minutes on high, 30 minutes on lower heat.

Recipe donated by Julie Wallinger, Souldrop

Smoked Bacon & Mushroom Risotto

2 tbsp olive oil
salt & ground black pepper
1 large onion, chopped
225g smoked streaky bacon, cut into strips
2 cloves garlic, crushed
1 red pepper, seeded & finely chopped

275g small courgettes, diced
175g button mushrooms, sliced
25g butter
250g risotto rice
50g Parmesan, grated
900mls hot chicken stock,
Chopped fresh parsley

- Heat the oil in a large non-stick frying pan, add the onion, garlic and red pepper, and sauté for a few minutes. Toss in the mushrooms and cook for a further minute.
- Add the rice and stir for 2 minutes. Pour in 750mls (25fl oz) of boiling stock and season.
- Cover with the lid and simmer until the rice is cooked – it should be soft on the outside but still have a little bite in the centre. Add more stock during this time if necessary.
- Fry and brown the bacon in a large non-stick frying pan. Remove and put onto a plate. Add the courgettes to the fat in the pan and fry until just tender. Put to one side with the bacon.
- Add the butter, grated parmesan, the bacon and courgettes to the cooked rice. Check the seasoning and serve sprinkled with chopped parsley and shavings of fresh Parmesan if liked. Serves 4-6.

Recipe donated by Kim Kelly, Souldrop

Spinach & Chicken "Cake"

Not really a cake at all, more of a mould.

8oz young spinach leaves
Salt & pepper
1 pint water
For the filling
1 medium onion
4oz button mushrooms
1oz butter

2 tsp chopped fresh oregano
or marjoram (only use 1 tsp
if using dried)
8oz cooked chicken
3 medium tomatoes
¼ medium cucumber
6oz Edam cheese
4 tbsp mayonnaise

- Wash and drain the spinach leaves. Cook in seasoned boiling water for approx 1 – 2 minutes. Drain very thoroughly and then use them to line a 9 inch sandwich time (or flan dish). Leave enough hanging over the edge to cover the top. Fry finely chopped onion, thinly sliced mushrooms and herbs in the butter until soft. Season and leave to cool. Chop chicken finely. Concass the tomatoes, put them briefly in boiling water and then skin them. Peel and finely slice the cucumber (you may want to save a few slices as garnish). Grate the cheese.

- Combine all of the filling ingredients with the mayonnaise and then use to fill the spinach lined mould. Cover with spinach leaves and leave to chill in the fridge for several hours.

- Turn out onto a plate, garnish if wished, and serve cut into slices like a cake.

Recipe donated by Eleanor, Souldrop.

Stuffed Chicken

4 boneless, skinless chicken breast fillets
4tsp maple syrup
6 ready to eat dried apricots
100g parma ham or rashers of smoked streaky bacon
125g pack goats cheese
300mls white wine
25g chopped walnuts

- Preheat oven to 190°C/170C (fan)/Gas 5.
- Split the fillets almost in half and open them out.
- Chop the apricots and mix with cheese and nuts.
- Spoon into the fillets and fold over.
- Drizzle each fillet with 1tsp maple syrup, wrap in the ham (or bacon) and transfer to a roasting dish.
- Pour the wine around the fillets. Roast for 30minutes, adding a splash of water to the dish if the wine evaporates.
- Transfer to a warm platter.
- Reheat the pan juices and pour over.
- Serve the chicken on top of the leeks with the pan juices. Serves 4.

Serve with creamed leeks and potato crush.
(see pages 74 & 79)

Recipe donated by Carol Mead, Souldrop

Tandoori Chicken

8 chicken legs or breasts

1-2 tsp lemon juice

Salt to taste

1/2 oz finely grated ginger

3 cloves of garlic very finely chopped

1 tsp ground coriander

1 tsp ground cumin

1 tsp chilli power (or leave out if you don't like chilli)

1 tsp paprika

1 tsp garam masala

1/2 tsp ground black pepper

1/4 pint of natural yoghurt (not low fat)

- Skin the chicken legs or breasts, wash thoroughly and dry on kitchen paper. Slash them with a sharp knife.
- Rub the lemon juice and salt on the slashed chicken pieces.
- Blend the ginger, and garlic in a blender with 1 tablespoon of water then mix the coriander, cumin, chilli powder, paprika, garam masala and pepper. Transfer the paste in large bowl and stir in the yoghurt.
- Add the chicken to this spiced yoghurt mix and making sure the chicken is covered in this paste. Cover with cling film and leave in the fridge overnight to marinate.
- Lay the chicken on the rack across the roasting tin and cook in the oven at 400F for about 45 minutes, until tender.
- Serve with an onion salad (mix of finely sliced onions, tomatoes, lettuce, lemon juice) and warm pitta bread. Serves 4.

Please note this can also be cooked on a barbeque.

Recipe donated by Paulina Chakravarthi, Souldrop

Tartiflette

1.5kg medium sized potatoes
1 large onion
200g diced smoked bacon or lardons
1 Reblochon cheese (usually bought as a semi-circle)
The Reblochon is best allowed to mature a little, but be warned
- it is a strong smelling cheese!
1 glass French white wine
300mls crème fraiche
25g butter

- Cook the potatoes in lightly salted water for 15 mins.
- Drain & allow to cool, then peel & slice into thick slices.
- While cooking the potatoes, peel and dice the onion, and fry over a medium heat for about 5 mins.
- Add the diced bacon and cook well for another 5 mins. The onion and bacon need to be slightly coloured.
- Smear some butter around a gratin dish.
- Layer half of the potatoes on the bottom of the dish.
- Cover the potatoes with half the onion & bacon mixture.
- Layer the remaining potatoes on top of that.
- Cover the potatoes with the remaining bacon & onion mixture.
- Spread the crème fraiche over the top.
- Halve the Reblochon lengthwise to give two thinner semi-circles of cheese. Keep the wax on the cheese & lay both halves on top of the dish to give a good spread.
- Pour a glass of wine over the top of the dish.
- Cook at 200C for about 10 minutes and then lower the heat to 180C until the cheese melts and browns on the surface. The cheese should melt into the dish and the fat drips down to crisp the potatoes.
- Serve hot with a green salad. Serves 4-6.

Variations: try using different wines; try substituting Reblochon with Brie; try using cream instead of crème fraiche. Garlic can be added to the onions as desired.

Recipe donated by Nina & Mick Chivers, Souldrop

Thai Red Duck Curry

2 tbsp vegetable oil

675g (1 lb 8 oz) duck (breast and thigh), sliced

12 shallots, thinly sliced

6 cloves garlic, finely chopped

2 tbsp fresh ginger, grated

75g (3 oz) Thai red curry paste

2 x 400mls cans coconut milk

1 tbsp soft brown sugar

3 kaffir (lime leaves), thinly sliced

2 tbsp lime juice

20 fresh basil leaves, ripped

3 handfuls washed spinach

1 tbsp fish sauce (nam pla)

1 bunch coriander leaves

1 bunch spring onions, trimmed and thinly sliced

2 green chillies, deseeded & sliced

- Heat the oil in a frying pan and brown the duck all over. Remove the meat from the pan and set aside.
- Add the shallots and garlic to the pan and cook over a medium heat until the onions start to brown.
- Add the ginger and curry paste and cook for 3 minutes, stirring continuously.
- Return the duck to the pan and add one can of coconut milk, the sugar and the lime leaves. Cook over a low heat for about 40 minutes until the beef is tender. The sauce will have split (curdled), but this is normal.
- Add the remaining can of coconut milk, lime juice, basil leaves, spinach and nam pla and cook for a further 5 minutes, stirring to combine.
- Garnish with the coriander, spring onions and chillies and serve with fragrant rice such as jasmine. Serves four.

Recipe donated by Mark Kelly, Souldrop

Tipsy Topside

2lb topside, cubed, 2"x 1/2 "
1tsp tomato puree
½ oz butter
½ pt stock
1 tbsp oil
2 tbsp cornflour
1 bunch spring onions, sliced
¼ bottle red wine
4 oz button mushrooms, sliced

- Preheat oven 180°, Gas 4.
- Brown meat in butter /oil and place in casserole.
- Fry onions and mushrooms in remaining fat and add to meat.
- Mix together tomato puree and stock. Pour over meat.
- Blend cornflour with a little water and add to casserole, stirring all the time.
- Stir in half the wine and cook for 1 ½ - 2 hours. Add the rest of the wine 10 minutes before serving.

PS You can substitute cider or beer for wine.

Recipe donated by Jann Horton, Souldrop

Souldrop Village, 1924.
Village Hall and Bedford
Arms Pub to right of picture.

All Saints Church Souldrop, October
2009. The Old church partly fell at
Christmas in 1795 and was rebuilt in
1800 by Mr Robert Salmon, funded
by John, the 6th Duke of Bedford. In
1860 – 1861, it was again rebuilt at
the cost of the 8th Duke of Bedford.

A sad photo of the old Bedford Arms
Pub ablaze in 1969. The boy on the
far left is Jeremy Viewing who still
lives in the village.

The Bedford Arms, Souldrop.

The Bedford Arms, with the original thatched roof – approx 1895.

Morris Men at Bedford Arms Souldrop, July 2009.

All Saints Church, Souldrop. Reverend Roberts Evens conducts the service every Sunday, at 9.00am, everyone welcome.

Cheesey Peppers

3 peppers of mixed colours	**500mls** semi-skimmed milk
1 large onion	**40g** cornflour
250g smoked bacon (optional)	**1 tsp** course grain mustard
250g mushrooms, sliced	**25g** butter
300g cheddar cheese, grated	Fresh parsley & slice of tomato for garnish
200g long grain rice	
1 clove garlic, finely chopped	Salt & pepper to season

- Cut off the tops of the peppers. Remove the stalk & seeds. Cut the peppers into medium sized (2cm) squares. Boil them in water for 10 minutes then drain.
- Rinse the rice for a minute under cold water, boil in salted water for 15 mins or according to instructions.
- While the rice is cooking, peel & dice the onion, & fry in the butter with the bacon in a large frying pan or wok over a medium heat for about 5 minutes.
- Add the garlic, sliced mushrooms & mustard & cook well for another 5 minutes.
- Remove from the heat & add the cornflour.
- Gradually stir in the milk & then return to medium heat.
- Continue to stir until the mixture thickens & boils.
- Stir in ¾ of the cheese until blended & season to taste.
- Add the cooked peppers and stir in.
- Add the cooked rice and stir in.
- Pour the mixture into an oven proof dish & cover with the remaining cheese.
- Add slices of tomato.
- Place under a medium-hot grill until the cheese melts & browns.
- Serve hot. Can be served on its own, or as an accompaniment to sausages.

This recipe has changed within the family over the years as different people have expressed different tastes & dislikes. It started off as stuffed peppers & could easily be reverted to its original form by omitting the peppers & using the rest of the mix to stuff them instead. This is the current format!

Recipe donated by Nina and Mick Chivers, Souldrop

Cheesy Potatoes Dauphinois

1lb potatoes - Desiree, King Edwards
or the like - thinly sliced
1 large onion, thinly sliced
150 mls double cream
150 mls milk
4 oz grated cheese
1 oz butter
Salt & fresh milled black pepper

- Gently cook onion until soft but not brown.
- In a greased gratin dish layer the potatoes
  and onion seasoning each layer finishing with
  potatoes neatly arranged on top.
- Mix together the cream, milk and half the cheese,
  pour over potatoes and dot butter on top.
- Bake in a pre-heated oven 150 deg C for about
  1 hour, remove and sprinkle remaining cheese on
  top and return to oven for another 30 minutes.
- Best served straight from oven when top is
  golden brown.

Good with fish, chicken or anything you like really.

Recipe donated by Angela Edmonds, Souldrop

Souldrop Vegetarian Dishes

Corn On The Cob

Corn on the cob
olive oil
Cajun spice

- Boil the corn on the cobs in the microwave. 10-12 minutes for two.
  They are sure to be cooked if the water starts to turn cloudy.
- Pour olive oil onto a plate, enough to cover half the plate.
  Sprinkle Cajun spice onto the oil.
- Take the corn on the cob out of the boiling water, roll it in the oil & eat it!
- Leave the remaining cobs in the water to keep them hot.
- You can sprinkle on the olive oil, your favourite spices or herbs.

Recipe donated by Robert Freeman, Souldrop

Creamed Leeks

2 leeks, trimmed and sliced
2 tbsp Crème Fraiche

- Put the leeks in pan with enough salted water to just
  cover. Cook for 10 minutes.
- Drain and return to the pan with the crème fraiche.
- Season and heat through.
- Serve with Stuffed chicken (See page 65). Serves 4.

Recipe donated by Carol Mead, Souldrop

Easy Tomato
& Goat's Cheese Tart

Pack of puff pastry
Fresh pesto
Fresh tomatoes – sliced
Goat's cheese sliced
Fresh thyme

- Preheat oven to 200°.
- Roll out puff pastry into rectangle – same size as a baking tray.
- Score around the pastry – 1cm from edge.
- Cover inside of score line with pesto.
- Lay tomato slices over pesto, overlapping.
- Cover with slices of goat's cheese.
- Sprinkle with herbs.
- Bake for 35 minutes.

A great store-cupboard starter or light lunch.

Recipe donated by the Johnson family, Souldrop

Souldrop Vegetarian Dishes

Glazed Carrots

1 ½ lb carrots (peeled)	**2 tbsp** sugar
2 oz butter	**2 tbsp** mixed herbs

- Cut the carrots into strips and cook in boiling water for 10 minutes. Drain well.
- Heat the butter and add the sugar and lightly brown. Add the herbs & carrots & continue cooking over a low heat for 10-15 minutes until the carrots are tender and glazed.

Recipe donated by Jenny Briggs, Souldrop. This was one of her mother's recipes

Hot Potato Salad

As tested on Mandy and Beth many years ago.

1 lb new potatoes	**4 tbsp** white wine vinegar
1 large onion	**1 tbsp** tarragon vinegar
1 green pepper	**2 tbsp** chopped spring onions
4 tbsp olive oil	**2 tbsp** chopped gherkins

- Cook the potatoes and slice once cool.
- Peel and chop the onions, dice the pepper (discard the seeds).
- Fry the onions in the oil until they are soft. Pour in the vinegars and heat well.
- Add the potatoes and spring onions to the onion/vinegars mixture, add the pepper, gherkins and season to taste.
- Can be served with chopped celery and parsley as garnish.

Recipe donated by Eleanor, Souldrop

Greek Roast Potatoes

Potatoes	Mixed herbs
2-3 Cloves of Garlic	Olive oil

- Par boil the required number of small whole potatoes (or cut larger ones to an even size), for about 10 mins.
- Drain and toss them firmly in the lidded pan to fluff up the surface.
- Place in a roasting tin with 2 or 3 cloves of garlic mixed herbs and olive oil.
- Cook until golden brown for about 1 hour at Gas mark 7/200°C/425F.
- Serve with Jenny's five hour lamb. (see page 52)

Recipe donated by Jenny Deacon, Souldrop

Kay's Egg Fried Special Rice

Frozen or refrigerated basmati rice (pre cooked)	**1 dsp** soy sauce
Thai seven spice	Ginger
2 eggs	Prawns
Salt & pepper	**2 spring onions**

- Heat Chinese oil in pan. Add egg, soy sauce and stir.
- Add frozen or refrigerated rice and stir continually.
- Add prawns and chopped spring onion.
- Add Thai seven spice, ginger and salt and pepper.
- Stir well and serve with Kay's chicken and cashew nuts with sweet and sour sauce. (see page 45)

Kay's tip – It has taken me a long time to be able to cook rice that is not stodgy and starchy. I believe the secret is precooking it first, rinsing well, then freezing or cooling.

Recipe donated by Kay Bone, Souldrop.

Souldrop Vegetarian Dishes

Leek & Stilton Bread & Butter Pudding

2 cloves of garlic
8 leeks sliced and washed
8oz mushrooms sliced
Oil for cooking
8-10 oz stilton (to taste)
Salt & pepper
Mixed herbs
3 eggs
1 pint milk
8-10 slices of bread and butter (depending on dish size)

- Place leeks, onions, mushrooms, garlic, mixed herbs, salt, pepper & oil in a pan.
- Sauté, cooking without colour.
- Place half the leek mixture in a deep dish.
- Lay half the bread and butter on top.
- Add the other half of the leek mixture on top, along with half the stilton.
- Place the rest of the bread on the top.
- Mix the egg and milk and pour over the top.
- Slice the remaining stilton and place on top.
- Bake in oven on gas mark 6 for 15-20 minutes or until the egg mixture has set.
- Cover with foil if it starts to burn – dull side on top.

Recipe donated by Sally,
The Bedford Arms Pub in Souldrop

Mixed Roast Vegetables

red, yellow & green peppers	red onion
carrot	small vine tomatoes
courgettes	olive oil.

- Cut red, yellow and green peppers into even chunks and arrange in shallow ovenproof dish.
- Add par boiled carrot sticks, sliced courgettes, sliced red onion.
- Top with small vine tomatoes.

- Drizzle with olive oil.
- Cook for 1 hour at gas mark 7/200°C/425°F until golden brown or about 1 hour.
- Serve with Jenny's five hour lamb. (see page 52)

Recipe donated by Jenny Deacon, Souldrop

Potato Crush

8 smallish potatoes	**1 tsp** paprika
2 tbsp olive oil	**1 tsp** herbes de province

- Preheat oven to 190°C/170°C(fan)/Gas 5.
- Boil the potatoes in their skins for 20 minutes or until just tender. Drain and transfer to roasting tin.
- Crush each one with a masher, drizzle with oil & sprinkle with the paprika and herbs.

- Bake for 25–30 minutes until golden.
- Serve as an accompaniment to stuffed chicken. (See page 65). Serves 4.

Recipe donated by Carol Mead, Souldrop

Roast Onions with Cheese

8 small red or brown onions
2tbsp olive oil
100mls cider - dry is best
25g butter
150g cheese - Brie is a good choice

- Preheat oven to 190C gas mark 5.
- Peel onions leaving base on so they sit well in the dish and cut a cross in the top of each one approx 3 quarters of the way down.
- Brush with the oil and put in roasting tin with left over oil. Put some butter in cross on each onion and pour the cider on top.
- Cover with foil and cook for 30 minutes.
- Remove the foil and baste and return onions to the oven without foil and cook for approx 25 minutes, basting occasionally.
- Put a piece of cheese on each onion and cook until the cheese melts.

This is a healthy vegetarian meal, nice served with crusty or naan bread or a selection of other roast vegetables.

Recipe donated by Sue Harwick, Souldrop

Spicy Potato Wedges

4 baking potatoes, (preferably Maris Pipers)
¼ level tsp cumin
3-4 tbsp oil – any kind you prefer
1 level tsp smoked paprika
¼ level tsp hot chilli powder
sea salt & freshly ground pepper

- Preheat the oven to 200°C/Gas mark 6 and prepare the potatoes. Wash them thoroughly and cut each potato into thick wedges.
- Pour the oil into a large bowl and toss the potato wedges in it.
- Combine the spices, pepper, and plenty of salt in a small bowl and then put half the mixture into a large plastic bag.
- Tip half the potato wedges into the bag and shake it energetically until the wedges are lightly dusted.
- Repeat with the other half.
- Arrange the wedges on an oiled baking tray.
- Cook for about 50 minutes, turning about half way through.
- Serve immediately with bonfire night chicken (see page 41).

Recipe donated by Caroline Rich, Souldrop

Tortilla

My Mum used to call this dish "Spanish omelette"
— as if there were no other, and quite frankly, who am I to argue!

Add things if you wish, but this is pure authentic tortilla as it was meant to be.
Para dos (for two)
3 free range eggs (medium)
1 onion (medium)

3 potatoes (medium & preferably of the old variety)
Olive oil (good quality but not necessarily extra virgin)
Sea salt & black pepper

- Slice the potatoes in a random fashion turning the potato as you do so. You want the cuts to be slightly wedge shaped and not too thin. Cut the onion in half and slice along the length.

- In a frying pan (size is down to whether you want the tortilla to be thick or thin), pour in enough oil to amply cover the bottom (don't scrimp on this, more is better than not enough), and season with salt, adding pepper if you wish (I do).

- Cooking the potatoes and onions isn't difficult, but don't have the oil too hot or everything will fry and become crisp, making the onion bitter and the potato like a chip. You want to be able to cook the onion and potato slowly, so that they become infused by the flavours of the seasoned oil, so take your time, turning the onions and potatoes occasionally so that everything cooks evenly.

- Beat your eggs into a bowl (large enough to add your potatoes and onions to) and add salt, and again pepper if you wish, to taste.

- When your onions and potatoes have become soft and golden, drain them from the oil and add to the egg. Keeping the heat under the pan, spoon in some of the oil you have just drained and add the tortilla mix, shaking it around the pan so that it cooks evenly. Cook until the bottom is firm and then flip onto a plate before placing back into the pan to cook the other side.

Tortilla is beautiful hot or cold, as a main dish or as part of tapas. However you serve it I hope you enjoy.

Recipe donated by Mari and Joe Zafar, Souldrop

Vegetable risotto

250 g Risotto rice
2 tbsp olive oil
1 or 2 onions
1 glass white wine (optional)
1.5 L vegetable or poultry stock - if you use wine, reduce volume of stock by amount of the wine
1 or 2 carrots

Vegetables ad lib, eg mushrooms, peppers, spinach, green soya beans, courgettes...
1 small bunch of flat leaf parsley or ½ pack frozen parsley
Grated parmesan
Butter

- Peel and chop onions.
- Wash and clean vegetables. Grate or cut carrots in fine strips, slice mushrooms, cut all other veg in small cubes, finely chop parsley.
- Boil 1.5 l water, make stock, put lid on and keep simmering in a separate pot.
- Heat olive oil to medium heat in a large heavy pot and sweat onions.
- Pour in rice and roast with onions until rice turns slightly transparent.
- Pour in white wine and/or a bit if the hot stock, add all cut veg and cover with stock.
- Now the tedious part: keep stirring (to avoid risotto sticking to pot and burning) and keep adding stock to always keep risotto slightly covered with liquid as the rice soaks the liquid up. Occasionally taste a few rice grains to check cooking progress.
- The risotto is done when the rice is soft; you can sometimes see a fine white line in the middle of each corn. This is normally the case when all stock is used up - after about 20 minutes. If you need more liquid, add small amounts of stock.
- Nearly there! Now take pot off the heat, add chopped parsley, parmesan (ad lib - my ideal amount is 80 – 100 g) and butter (again ad lib - I use 30 – 50 g). Now stir vigorously for about a minute to mix in the rice starch - you'll see the risotto turn creamy. Season with pepper- you should not need any extra salt.
- Done!

Recipe donated by Angela & Christof Schloesser, Souldrop

Landscape view over
Cross Weir Farm, 1960's.

High Street, Souldrop, looking
over the field to Church farm
and the Old Church Farm.

The Old Post Office which is
now a residential property.

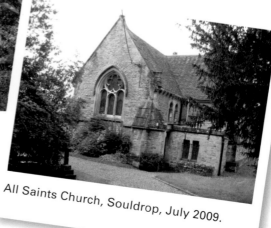

All Saints Church, Souldrop, July 2009.

Cross Weir Farm, working farm until 2000.

The Old Church Farm – looking from the front view in the High Street. This was sold by the Gullivers and is now a residential property,

Three Grade 2 listed cottages, which used to house the farm workers.

All Saints Church, Souldrop, July 2009.

Souldrop Desserts

Apple and Blackberry Crumble

2 large apples
6oz sugar
Cupful of blackberries
4oz margarine
4oz self raising flour

- Peel, core and thinly slice apples.
- Wash blackberries.
- Put them all in a Pyrex dish and sprinkle with 2ozs of the sugar.
- Cover with cling film and cook for 5 minutes in microwave or until slightly soft.
- Make crumble with margarine, flour and rest of sugar. Mix with your fingers until it resembles breadcrumbs. Spread it evenly on top of the fruit.
- Bake for 20-25 minutes on Gas Mark 5 (180°C) until golden brown.
- Serve with custard, ice cream or cream.

Recipe donated by Daphne Papworth, Souldrop

Apple Charlotte

4 oz fresh breadcrumbs
2 oz butter
5oz brown sugar
1 tbsp lemon juice
1 ½ lb cooking apples
2 tbsp water

- Heat oven to 200°C/400°F/Gas 5.
- Grease 1½ lb pie dish.
- Mix breadcrumbs & brown sugar together.
- Peel, core and slice apples & arrange in layers in pie dish.
- Spread breadcrumb mixture over apples in a thick layer.
- Press well with knuckles into dish.
- Melt butter & mix with lemon juice and water.
- Pour over breadcrumbs & bake for 40 minutes near the top of the oven.

The recipe is a family favourite, belonging to Mrs C.E. Smith.

Recipe donated by Sheila and Ken Smith, Souldrop

Apple Pan Dowdy

4 large cooking apples, peeled, cored & sliced

2 tbsp brown sugar

2 tbsp golden syrup

1 tsp nutmeg

4oz self-raising flour

pinch salt

2oz sugar

1 beaten egg

4 tbsp milk

2oz melted butter

- Put the prepared apples in a deep, greased dish with the brown sugar, golden syrup and nutmeg.
- Cover with a lid or tinfoil and bake on a medium heat for 15 minutes, or until the apples are soft.
- Meanwhile, sieve together the flour, sugar and salt. Gradually beat in the egg, milk and melted butter to make a smooth batter. Spoon over the apples.
- Bake for a further 30-35 minutes (180degrees C = 350 degrees F = mark 4) or until top is golden brown.
- Test the batter with a knife. If the knife comes clean, it's done.
- Eat.

Eat a second helping – with cream or custard, if you can bear all the calories.

Recipe donated by Karen Godden, Souldrop

Apple Spice Cake

12oz plain flour
2tbsp water
3 level tsp baking powder
2 level tbsp golden syrup
3 level tsp mixed spice
1 tsp lemon juice
½ level tsp ground ginger
1 eating apple sliced

8oz dark brown sugar
3 level tbsp golden syrup
12 oz eating apples, peeled and grated
Grated rind of ½ a lemon
7fl. oz. sunflower oil
3 eggs, size 3
(**8 ½ inch** spring clip tin, based, lined and greased).

- Set oven to moderate, gas mark 4 or 350°F/180°C (160° fan oven).
- Sift together flour, baking powder and spices. Stir in sugar, apples and lemon rind. Make a well in the centre.
- Beat the oil, eggs and syrup together and pour into the well in the flour. Use a wooden spoon to draw the flour into the liquid. Beat thoroughly.
- Pour the cake into a tin. Bake in the centre of the oven for approximately 1 ¼ hours or until the cake springs back when gently touched. Leave to cool.
- To make the topping: put the water, golden syrup and lemon juice in a frying pan. Place the apple slices in a single layer in the pan. Poach gently for 2 minutes and remove. Bring the liquid to the boil and reduce by half. Arrange the apple slices on the cake and brush with glaze.

Recipe donated by Carol Mead, Souldrop

Apricot Upside-Down Tart

For the pastry
(or one pack of ready
made sweet pastry)
235g plain flour
Pinch salt
170g chilled unsalted butter,
cut into cubes
50g caster sugar
1 large egg,
beaten with **1 tbsp** water

Butterscotch filling
100g caster sugar
(**+ 1 tsp** for dusting)
50mls water
55g butter
8 medium apricots
(fresh, halved and stoned)

- Preheat oven to 200°.
- Pastry – blend flour and salt in food processor. Add butter and sugar and blend again until breadcrumb texture.
- With motor running, add enough egg and water to form a dough.
- Turn out dough onto large sheet of baking paper and cover with another sheet of paper. Roll out to 25cm diameter and trim to a neat circle.
- Butterscotch – heat sugar and water in small, ovenproof frying pan over low heat for 2-3 minutes – until resembling syrup.
- Increase heat and simmer for 4-5 minutes until caramelised (do not stir, just swirl pan).
- Remove from heat and add 40g butter – stir until smooth and thick. Leave for 5 minutes.
- Place apricots cut side down in warm butterscotch.
- Cover pan with pastry circle and tuck in edges. Prick all over with fork and dot with butter and sprinkle with 1tsp sugar.
- Bake for 25 – 30 minutes, or until golden brown.
- Turn out and serve with cream or ice cream – delicious warm or cold.

Recipe donated by the Johnsons, Souldrop

Baked Cheesecake

Filling	Base
750g Philadelphia cream cheese	**250g** Sweet digestive biscuits
½ cup Caster sugar	**125g** Butter
3 Eggs	
3 tsp Grated lemon rind	
¼ cup Lemon juice	

- Melt the butter and crush the biscuits finely, mix these together until all the biscuit is coated with the butter. Press the mix into a flan dish and refrigerate.
- To make the filling, beat the cheese and sugar together with a wooden spoon and add the eggs one at a time beating well between each addition.
- Add the rind and lemon juice and beat until creamy.
- Taste to ensure desired sweetness. Add more sugar to taste.
- Pour the mixture over the cooled biscuit mix and bake in a moderately slow oven (160°C) for about 50 minutes.
- After 50 minutes do not open the door - switch off the oven and leave with the door shut for a few hours or even overnight to prevent cracking.
- When completely cool, place in the fridge to chill before serving.

This traditional Devonshire recipe is a family favourite. It was given to me by my aunt who has lived in Devon for the last 15 years.

Recipe donated by Jenny Briggs, Souldrop

Souldrop Desserts

Baklava

Filo pastry
clear runny honey
6oz Chopped mixed nuts
3oz melted butter
2oz caster sugar
cloves
1 heaped tsp cinnamon

- Mix together sugar, cinnamon, nuts.
- Cut filo sheets to fit the dish (rectangular, approx 8"x5" is best).
- Spread four sheets of pastry with melted butter and layer in the base of the dish.
- Cover with a layer of the nut mixture.
- Add 3 sheets of buttered pastry, a layer of the nut mix etc, until the dish is full.
- Top with three sheets of buttered pastry.
- Mark the top of the baklava into triangles and place a clove in each section.
- Sprinkle the top with water and bake at 300°F for about 30 minutes, then at 350°F for another 20 minutes until golden brown.
- Pour over the warm honey and leave until cold and the honey is fully absorbed.
- If it is too sticky or hard, sprinkle it with water and leave for a few hours to soften.
- Serve as a dessert after Jenny's five hour lamb. (see page 52)

Recipe donated by Jenny Deacon, Souldrop

Banana and Toffee Delight

10 mini meringues
3 medium bananas, peeled and sliced
300mls of whipping cream
75g of pecan nuts, chopped
1 tbsp of icing sugar
200g of toffee sauce

- Break the meringues into large pieces.
- Lightly whip the cream until it's just fluffy, then add the icing sugar.
- Gently stir in the meringue, bananas and 2/3 of the nuts.
- Fold in four tbsp toffee sauce and spoon into four dessert glasses.
- Top with the remaining nuts and drizzle with the extra sauce.

Recipe donated by Kristy Mead, Souldrop

Souldrop Desserts

Beckie's Seasonal Berry Gooey Ooey Pudding
- easy blackberry fool*

160g/6oz blackberries
16 tbsp icing sugar
400mls/16fl oz double cream, whipped

- Preparation time - less than 30 minutes.
- Cooking time - no cooking required.
- Place the blackberries and icing sugar in a bowl and mash together with a fork.
- Add the cream and fold together.
- Transfer the mixture to a glass and serve**

*You can use any berry or a mixture of berries for this recipe, but as there is an abundance of blackberry bushes in Souldrop, it's nice to get out and forage and get "free- range / organic" food!

**You can also add crushed meringue to the bottom of the glass just before dishing out and it gives it a lovely crispy end to your pud. And finish the evening with a nice glass of port and coffee!

Recipe donated by Beckie Smith, Souldrop

Chilled Lemon Flan

4oz digestive biscuits, crushed
2oz butter
1 tbsp caster sugar
0.25 pt single cream
6oz condensed milk
2 large lemons

- Melt the butter in a pan, add crushed biscuits, sugar and stir.
- Put the biscuit mix in a flan dish, pressing down with the back of a wooden spoon against the base and sides of the flan dish.
- Bake in a slow oven for 8 minutes, then leave to cool.
- Mix the cream and condensed milk together, add juice & rind from the lemons and stir.
- Pour in to the cooled flan dish.
- Refrigerate for two hours.

Recipe donated by Amy Maddison, Souldrop

Chocolate Ice Cream

Rum and raisin ice cream (or flavour of your choice)
Mars bars (quantity used depending on number in company)
Nuts (crumbled mixture of nuts)

- Cut the Mars bars into small pieces.
- Melt in dish over a boiling pan. Stir gently until melted completely to a pouring consistency.
- Scoop ice cream into serving dishes.
- Pour the melted mars bars over the ice cream.
- The Mars bar mixture should set quickly so sprinkle the crumbled nuts on before it sets.

Recipe donated by Julie and Bob Hancock, Souldrop

Chocolate Roulade

4 eggs
6oz icing sugar
1 ½ oz cocoa
Filling
anything of your own choice.
eg **1/3 pt** cream (whipped) & strawberries or
8 individual chocolate mousses & raspberries or
toffee mousses & chopped nuts

- Line a 12 x 9" sandwich tin with greaseproof paper.
- Separate eggs.
- Work egg yolks, icing sugar and cocoa together by gradually sifting the icing sugar and cocoa and stirring into the egg yolks.
- Whisk egg whites until very stiff.
- Slowly fold the egg whites until very stiff into the chocolate mixture, a spoonful at a time.
- Pour into the prepared tin.
- Cook in a preheated oven gas no 7 (230°c) for 10 minutes - no more. Cake may still look quite soft.
- Turn onto floured greaseproof paper and peel off original tin lining paper using a palette knife immediately while the cake is still hot.
- Roll up with floured paper inside and wrap in a damp tea towel. Leave to cool.
- Unroll and fill sponge with filling of choice when cool. Roll back up and decorate with spare fruit, chocolate etc and dust with icing sugar.

Recipe donated by Susan, Souldrop

Souldrop Desserts

Elizabeth's Easy Pud

Equal quantities of Greek yoghurt and double cream
Frozen fruit
Demerara sugar

- Whip the cream and fold in the yoghurt.
- Put the frozen fruit in a dish and cover with the cream and yoghurt.
- Cover with Demerara sugar.
- Place uncovered in fridge and leave for a couple of days.
- It's as easy as that!

Recipe donated by Sylvia, Souldrop

Eve's Pudding

450g/1lb cooking apples, peeled and sliced.

75g/2 ¾ oz caster sugar

75g/ 2 ¾ oz granulated sugar

1 egg beaten

1 tbsp lemon juice

150g/5 ½ oz self raising flour

50g/1 ¾ oz sultanas

3 tbsp milk

75g/2 ¾ oz butter

25g/1oz flaked almonds

- Grease an 850mls/1 ½ pt ovenproof dish.
- Mix the apples with the sugar, lemon juice and sultanas, then spoon into the greased dish.
- Cream the butter and caster sugar together until pale and then gradually add the egg.
- Carefully fold in the self raising flour and stir in the milk to give a soft dropping consistency.
- Spread the mixture over the apples and sprinkle with the flaked almonds.
- Bake in a preheated oven 180°C/350°F, Gas mark 4, for 40-45 minutes until the sponge is golden brown.
- Serve hot with custard or double cream.

Recipe donated by Julie Venison, Souldrop

Forest Fruit Cakes

3 tbsp ground almonds

1½-2 tbsp good lemon curd

100g plain flour

200g forest fruit eg blueberries, currants, strawberries, raspberries

1 tbsp light brown soft sugar

Icing sugar to dust - optional

50g creamy butter cold, in small pieces

2 tbsp water

5 tbsp crème fraîche

6.5cm biscuit cutter

12" cake tin

- Put the ground almonds, sugar & the plain flour in a bowl & mix together.
- Then add the butter and rub it in.
- Add the water, and mix with a spoon until it becomes one or two big lumps of dough, (you may need to add extra water).
- Press the dough together like a ball & put it in the refrigerator for at least 30 minutes.
- Roll the dough on a lightly floured work surface.
- Cut about 12 dough circles with a biscuit cutter and place them in the greased cake tins.
- Make little holes on the bottom of the dough in the cake tins with a fork.
- Bake them for around 12 minutes on a 190 C oven, until the cakes are risen and golden.
- Allow to cool on a metal grid.
- Mix the crème fraîche & lemon curd in a bowl & add the mixture to the cakes.
- Add the fruit to the cakes and sprinkle with icing sugar (optional).

This dessert is our favorite!

Recipe donated by Esta, Hein, Sven and Femke Meiland, Souldrop

German Cheesecake

For the base
200g plain flour
3g baking powder
60g caster sugar
1 tsp vanilla sugar
1 egg
75g soft margarine

For the filling
cut apples or cherries
750g quark
120g caster sugar
2 tsp vanilla sugar
4 eggs
1 tsp lemon juice
250mls milk
100g potato flour
nuts, cinnamon, raisins

Base

- Mix altogether and knead into a paste.
- Work into a ball and put into fridge whilst making filling.

Filling

- Put potato flour, quark, sugar, vanilla essence, egg yolks and lemon juice in a bowl. Add milk, beat until smooth.
- Beat egg whites until stiff and fold into mixture. Add raisins.
- Place base into a buttered tin. Spread with apples or cherries, nuts and cinnamon and put quark mixture over all.
- Bake for 60 - 70 minutes at Gas 4.
  May need covering to prevent over-browning.

Recipe donated by Jann Horton, Souldrop

Souldrop Desserts

Hazelnut Meringue

4 egg whites	Pinch of cream of tartar
½ tsp vanilla essence	**8 fluid oz** double cream
8ozs caster sugar	**2 tsps** cornflour
4oz finely chopped hazelnuts	**8oz** raspberries

- Preheat oven to 140°C.
- Line 2 swiss roll tins with baking parchment and mark out a circle about 7" in diameter.
- Put egg whites in a mixing bowl & add cream of tartar.
- Whisk with an electric hand whisk on low speed.
- Continue until whites are foamy, then increase speed to medium and carry on whisking until egg whites reach the stiff – peak stage.
- Whisk the caster sugar in a tablespoon at a time, until the mixture is stiff and glossy.
- Whisk in the cornflour and vanilla essence.
- Finally, fold in the hazelnuts with a metal spoon.
- Divide mixture between the 2 tins and place in the lower and middle shelves of the oven.
- Cook for 50-60 minutes. Swap the tins around after about 30 minutes.
- Turn off oven, but leave meringues to dry out in the oven until it is completely cold.
- Whisk cream until stiff.
- Remove parchment from meringue and place on a decorative plate.
- Pile ½ the cream on this, then put on the raspberries, (or any summer fruits you favour).
- Pile the rest of the cream on second meringue & place carefully on the first layer.
- Chill in fridge until ready to serve.

Recipe donated by Rose Murray, Souldrop

Lime Meringue Roulade

5 egg whites
275g (10oz) caster sugar
50g (2oz) flaked almonds
Filling
300mls (10fl oz) double cream
grated rind & juice of **1** lime
2 generous tablespoons lime or lemon curd

- Line a 33 x 23cm (13 x 9 in) Swiss roll tin with greased non-stick paper. Secure the corners with paperclips or staple each corner.
- First make the meringue. Whisk the egg whites until very stiff. Gradually add the sugar, a teaspoon at a time, whisking well between each addition. Whisk until very shiny and all the sugar has been added.
- Spread the meringue mixture into the prepared tin & sprinkle with almonds.
- Cook the meringue in a pre-heated oven at 220C/425F/Gas mark 7 for about 12 minutes until golden. Then lower the oven temperature to 160C/325F/Gas mark 3 and bake for a further 15 minutes until firm to the touch.
- Remove the meringue from the oven and turn almond side down onto a sheet of non-stick paper. Remove the paper from the base of the cooked meringues and allow to cool for about 10 minutes.
- Lightly whip the cream, add the lime rind & juice, & fold in the lime or lemon curd. Spread evenly over the meringue. Make an indentation 1cm in on the long side with a knife, then roll up the meringue fairly tightly from the long end to form a roulade. It is essential to roll tightly & firmly at the beginning.
- Wrap in non-stick baking paper and chill well before serving – raspberries go well with this roulade. Makes 8-10 slices.

Recipe donated by Kim Kelly, Souldrop

The Old Post Office
Plum Upside Down Cake

Cake
3oz/75g butter
3oz/75g caster sugar
2 eggs
4oz/100g self raising flour
Drop of vanilla essence
Pinch of salt

Topping
Approx **8** juicy plums
2oz/50g butter
2oz/50g soft brown sugar

- Grease a 7 inch/18cm round cake tin.
- To prepare the topping – cream the butter & soft brown sugar until light & fluffy. Spread the mixture over the base of the tin.
- Halve and stone the plums & press, cut side down, into the topping mixture.
- Cream the butter & sugar together until light & fluffy.
- Add the beaten eggs one at a time & mix well into the creamed mixture.
- Sift the flour & salt & fold into the mixture using a metal spoon.
- Add the vanilla essence & a little warm water if mixture is too stiff.
- Spread the mixture evenly on top of the plums & smooth the top.
- Bake for 40 minutes at 190°/gas mark 5.
- Invert onto a plate & serve hot or cold.

Recipe donated by Pip Judge, Souldrop

Phoebe's Pudding

This is more of an assembly line than a recipe

Crushed meringue (quite large pieces)

Chocolate ice cream (Ben & Jerry's Phish Food is a favourite)

Fresh or frozen berries (I recommend raspberries)

Whipped cream

- Layer the first three ingredients, finishing with a (large) spoonful of cream.

Recipe donated by Eleanor, Souldrop

Railway Pudding

4oz flour
3oz sugar
2oz milk
1 ½ tsp baking powder

1 egg
1oz butter
1 pinch salt

- Mix flour, sugar and salt.
- Beat the egg and add to the mixture.
- Add the milk stirring the mixture to a creamy texture.
- Melt the butter & add to the mixture with baking powder.
- Pour mixture into a greased tin, and bake in a preheated oven at 150°C for 20 minutes.
- Divide & serve with golden treacle & /or custard.

Railway workers used to live in a camp in Souldrop, and this recipe was used as an "energy bar" to fuel them with basic ingredients.

Recipe donated by Jeremy Viewing, Souldrop

Raspberry and Kiwi Pavlova

6oz caster sugar

2tsp cornflour

3 egg whites

½ **tsp** vinegar

½ **tsp** vanilla essence

fresh raspberries & kiwi fruit

- Beat egg whites until stiff.
- Gradually add sugar whilst still whisking until shiny.
- Add vinegar, vanilla essence and cornflour –
  whisk for a few seconds.
- Cover a baking tray with non-stick paper. Place
  meringue mixture in centre of tray and, using a
  spoon, hollow out the middle to make a circle
  about 8 inches across.
- Put in oven until golden and crisp,
  usually lovely and gooey on inside.
- Bake at 140° for 50-60 minutes.
- When cold, add fresh raspberries and kiwi fruit.

Recipe donated by Julie Wallinger, Souldrop

Strawberry or Summer Fruit Mess

Meringue
6 Egg Whites
300g Sugar
1 tbsp of balsamic vinegar
or red wine vinegar

Filling
Double Cream
Strawberries or
any summer fruits
Box of Chocolate Flakes

(If you wish to make it chocolate meringue just add 3 tbsp of chocolate cocoa powder sieved and 50g of dark chocolate when adding the sugar)

To make the meringue

- Beat the egg whites together until they form soft peaks.
- Then beat in the sugar a spoonful at a time until the meringue is stiff & shiny.
- Add the vinegar & if making chocolate meringue sprinkle in the cocoa powder & the chopped dark chocolate.
- Gently fold everything together until the cocoa in completely mixed in.
- Turn out into a mound on a baking tray (covered with a baking sheet) in a large fat circle (approx 23cm).
- Put in the oven and cook for approximately 1 to 1 ¼ hours (at around gas mark 2 or 150).
- When it's ready it should be crisp around the edges & sides & dry on the top. Turn the oven off & leave the door open & allow the meringue disc to cool completely.

Putting it all together

- Once the meringue has cooled you simply gather all the ingredients & break it all up together into a large bowl.
- Then pour over the cream & give a slight stir.
- You can also grate dark chocolate over the top for a real chocolate feast.

It may not be the most attractive of dishes but it sure is tasty – enjoy!

NB If you are short on time you can cheat and buy meringue nests and break them up instead.

Recipe donated by Mari and Joe Zafar, Souldrop

Souldrop Desserts

Sue's Banoffee Pie with Pecans

This banoffee pie with pecans in the base is delicious!

For the caramel
100g/3½ oz unsalted butter
100g/3½ oz caster sugar
400g/14 fl oz can condensed milk

For the banoffee pie
150g/5oz digestive biscuits, crushed
230g/4oz pecans halved
75g/3oz butter, melted
3 large bananas, chopped

- For the caramel, place the butter and sugar into a non-stick pan over a low heat, stirring until the butter melts and the sugar dissolves.
- Add the condensed milk and slowly bring to the boil, stirring continuously, to make the caramel. As soon as the mixture thickens and begins to smell of caramel, remove from the heat and allow to cool.
- Meanwhile, place the crushed biscuits and the pecans into a bowl. Add the butter and mix well.
- Transfer the mixture to a 25cm/10in cake tin. Press to pack the mixture evenly into the base.
- Add the chopped bananas to the caramel mixture & mix well, then spread the mixture over the biscuit base.
- Transfer to the refrigerator to cool for 30 minutes.

Recipe donated by Sue Rogers, Souldrop

Tiramisu Ice-Cream Cake

2x250g tubs mascarpone
5 tbsp fresh ground coffee
115g caster sugar
85g caster sugar
6 tbsp marsala

3 tbsp brandy
50g dark chocolate/chopped
200g bag sponge finger
142mls tub double cream

- Line a 1 kg tin with cling film.
- Beat the mascarpone sugar and marsala together, and then fold in the chopped chocolate and cream.
- Make up the coffee with 600mls boiling water.
- After 5 minutes, strain into a bowl, then stir in the sugar and brandy.
- Quickly dip the biscuits, one at a time, into the coffee mixture and line them along the base and up the long sides of the tin.
- Spoon in half the creamy mixture.
- Dip two biscuits into the coffee, place on top, end to end.
- Spoon the remaining creamy mixture on top, putting any remaining biscuits on the top as a lid. Fold over the sponge fingers above the rim into the middle, and press lightly into filling.
- Cover and freeze.
- To serve, turn out onto a plate, strip off the cling film, allow 15 – 20 mins before slicing.
- Serve with grated chocolate pieces and/ or cocoa powder & extra cream.

When this desert is on the 'pudding board' it proves to be very popular, especially amongst the staff! it is a bit time consuming to make, but well worth it.

Recipe donated by The Bedford Arms, Souldrop

Toffee Apple Crumble

For the base	For the topping
125g Golden Syrup	**175g** SR Flour
50g Butter	**75g** Butter (cold)
120g Light brown sugar	Zest of lemon
½ tsp Vanilla essence	**75g** Light brown sugar
100mls Cream	**50g** Ground almonds
2 Cooking apples	

- Heat oven to 160°C.
- Mix the toffee ingredients in a pan and boil for 2-3 minutes, set aside.
- To make the topping, rub together the flour and butter until like breadcrumbs, and then add the other ingredients.
- Peel and core the apple, and then put that in the base of an oven proof dish. Pour the toffee mixture over it, and then cover with the crumble mixture.
- Bake for 30 minutes or until the topping is golden and the apples have softened.

Recipe donated by Jenny Briggs, Souldrop

Toffee Apple Pudding

Topping	Base
5oz self raising flour	**2** dessert apples
1 tsp baking powder	**1oz** butter
1 tsp ground mixed spice	**1oz** light brown sugar
4oz soft margerine	**3 ½ oz** hard toffee
4oz caster sugar	**2 – 4 tbsp** milk
2 tbsp milk	
2 eggs	

- Grease a 2 pt pudding basin.
- Sift flour, baking powder and spice in a bowl.
- Add margarine, sugar, eggs. Beat all together.
- Gradually stir in some milk. Leave on one side.
- Topping – peel, core and thinly slice eating apples.
- Melt butter in a pan. Add brown sugar.
- Heat gently and stir until all sugar is dissolved.
- Stir in apple slices, gently warm for 1 minute.
- Arrange apple slices in greased basin, overlapping.
- Reserve butter mix in pan for sauce.
- Spoon sponge mix over apples in basin, smooth top, cover tightly with foil.
- Stand basin in small roasting tin, in 1" of water
- Bake in oven 190°C for approx 50 minutes, until well risen and firm.

- Meanwhile, break up toffee or unwrap separate toffees and add to butter mix in a pan.
- Heat gently, stirring to prevent sticking until dissolved, then stir in enough milk to make a smooth sauce.
- Run a knife around the edge of the sponge and invert onto a warm plate.
- Pour over the sauce.
- Serve with custard or cream

Nancy's hint – we often make double the quantity of sauce to serve separately.

Recipe donated by Nancy Mills, Souldrop

Back Lane, Souldrop, July 2009.

Back Lane, Souldrop, leading up to the railway bridge, July 2009.

Old Church Farm, October 2009.

Back Lane, with Gulliver's Spinney, to left of picture, July 2009.

Looking over the railway line northbound and the beautiful countryside next to Railway Cottage, Back Lane, Souldrop, July 2009.

Souldrop Countryside.

Looking over the splendid views of Souldrop, July 2009.

Views of Souldrop.

Old Church Farm, October 2009.

Looking over the other side of the railway line southbound and the panoramic views, Back Lane, Souldrop, July 2009.

Souldrop Cakes & Biscuits

Banana Cake

4 oz butter
4 oz sugar
2 eggs - whisked
2 over-ripe mashed bananas
1 **level tsp.** bicarbonate of soda
2 **tbsp** boiling milk
1 **tsp**. baking powder
8 oz plain Flour

- Cream together butter and sugar.
- Add eggs, mashed bananas then
  the soda dissolved in the milk.
- Lastly, add flour and baking powder previously
  sifted together. I usually do this in the food processor
  - it's less time consuming!
- Bake in two greased 7-inch sandwich tins for 20
  minutes @ 350 degrees F. You can also bake in a cake
  tin then slice in half afterwards (that's what I do).
- Fill with whipped double cream and sliced bananas.

Recipe donated by Kim Kelly, Souldrop

Boiled Fruit Cake

500g dried fruit
2 large eggs beaten
450mls water
150g plain flour
115g butter
150g self-raising flour
2 tbsp golden syrup

½ tsp mixed spice
150g dark brown sugar
½ tsp nutmeg
1 tsp bicarbonate of soda
1 tsp vanilla essence
1 tbsp boiling water

- Sift flour and spices together.
- Heat water, dried fruit, butter, golden syrup
  and brown sugar until simmering.
  Take off heat and allow to cool slightly.
- Add flour, spices, beaten eggs
  and vanilla essence. Stir.
- Mix bicarbonate of soda with hot water
  and put into mixture and stir well.
- Pour into 2lb lined loaf tin.
- Bake in centre of oven at 350°F for about 1 hour.

Recipe donated by Fran Simms, Souldrop

Souldrop Cakes & Biscuits

Celebration Cake

4 oz butter	**2 tsp** mixed spice
8 oz caster sugar	**1** individual plain yoghurt – about 125 grams
2 large eggs - beaten	
9 oz plain flour	Icing
1 tsp bicarbonate of soda	**3 oz** butter
1 tsp salt	**8 oz** icing sugar
1 tsp cinnamon	**2 tbs** milk

- Cream butter and sugar.
- Add alternately flour and beaten eggs. Start and finish with flour.
- Add soda, salt and spices, then mix in yoghurt.
- Preheat oven to 350F/180C. Grease and line two 7" sandwich tins.
- Spread mix into tins and cook for 20 - 25 minutes - slightly less if fan oven - or until springy to the touch in the centre.
- Cool on trays.
- Mix and ice both tops, sandwich together.

Recipe donated by Debbie, Souldrop

Chocolate Brownies

1lb granulated sugar

3oz cocoa

6oz self- raising flour + ½ **tsp** salt

4 med eggs beaten together with **4 tbsp** of milk

½ lb melted butter

6oz chopped walnuts or chopped, toasted hazelnuts or mixture of both.

6oz raisins

1 large bar good quality plain chocolate, chopped into small pieces.

- Use a large roasting tin – remember to line with parchment paper.
- Melt butter in a small pan and mix in the sugar.
- In a mixing bowl mix in flour, cocoa, nuts & raisins.
- Add beaten egg mixture.
- Fold in chopped plain chocolate.
- Cook in medium oven for about 20- 30 minutes or until the top springs back when touched – do not overcook!

If cooking in the Aga put the baking plate in the top and cook in the middle of top oven.

Recipe donated by Sally Bartlett, Souldrop

Chocolate Cake

3 eggs
1 tsp baking powder
2-4 tbsp water
Same weight as the 3 eggs of:
Butter
Sugar
Self raising flour
(remove 1 – 2 tbsp flour and replace with cocoa)

- Weigh the eggs and then weigh out the same amount of butter and sugar.
- Add all the ingredients into a mixer and mix well.
- Mixture should fall off a spoon.
- Pour into 2 well greased tins.
- Bake for 20 – 25 minutes at 180°C or on a baking shelf. on the floor of the bottom right of a four door Aga.
- The sides of the cake should be just leaving the tin.
- Put butter icing in between the two layers and on top of the cake.
- Eat as soon as possible.

Recipe donated by Chamberlaynes, Souldrop

Christmas Cookies

175g/6oz/ ¾ cup unsalted butter
5mls/ 1tsp vanilla essence
300g/11oz/1 ½ cups caster sugar
grated rind of 1 lemon
1 egg
pinch of salt
1 egg yolk
300g/11oz/2 ½ cups of plain flour
Coloured icing and small sweets, eg coloured silver balls, coloured silver crystals to decorate

- Beat butter with an electric mixer until soft. Gradually add sugar and continue beating until light and fluffy.
- Gradually mix in the whole egg and egg yolk, using a wooden spoon.
- Sift the flour over the mixture and stir to blend. Gather dough into a ball, wrap and chill for 30 minutes.
- Preheat oven to 190°C/375°F/Gas 5. Remove the dough from the refrigerator & unwrap, then roll out onto a lightly floured surface until about 3mm/1/8 in thick.
- Stamp out shapes, such as Christmas trees, crescents and stars with floured biscuit (cookie cutters). Alternatively, stamp out plain round cookies.
- Bake for about 8 minutes until lightly coloured. Transfer the cookies to a wire rack with a palette knife or metal spatula. Leave to cool completely before decorating, with icing and sweets.

Recipe donated by Jonathan Viewing, Souldrop,
who makes these at the end of term

Cornflake Cakes

25g / 1oz sugar
8 squares chocolate
2 cups cornflakes
50g / 2oz margarine
1 tbsp golden syrup

- Melt margarine, sugar and syrup in a pan.
- Remove from heat, add chocolate and stir.
- Add cornflakes and stir.
- Spoon into cake cases and put in the fridge to set.

Recipe donated by Amy Maddison, Souldrop

Crackle Cakes

1oz (25g) sugar
1oz (25g) butter
2 tbsp cocoa
1 tbsp golden syrup or honey
1oz (25g) cornflakes
To decorate
Coloured chocolate drops

- Put the sugar, cocoa, golden syrup or honey into a pan over low heat. Stir until the ingredients have melted.
- Stir the cornflakes into the mixture until they are completely coated.
- Spoon a little of the mixture into each of the paper cases. Top each with a coloured chocolate drop and leave them to set.

Clare used to make these with Sean when they were younger and has made some today. They were very tasty and Clare is sure that Sean would enjoy them as they have chocolate in, which he loved.

Recipe donated by Clare Bone, Souldrop (Sean's sister)

Flapjacks

(Sean's favourite — he would eat the lot!)

4oz. Butter
1oz soft brown sugar
4tbsp golden syrup
8oz rolled oats

- Melt butter, sugar and syrup in a large pan or in a bowl in the microwave.
- Add oats and mix well.
- Spread mixture into a greased 20x30cms (8x12 inches) tin.
- Bake in centre of a preheated oven for 20 minutes or until golden brown and firm to touch.
- Mark into squares or fingers while warm.
- Leave to cool in the tin and remove carefully. Makes 18 – 24. Enjoy!

Recipe donated by Kay Bone, Souldrop (Sean's Mum)

Ginger Shortcake

Biscuits	Icing
4oz butter	**4 level tbsp** sifted icing sugar
2oz caster sugar	**2oz** butter
5oz plain flour	**1 level tsp** ground ginger
1 level tsp baking powder	**3 level tsp** golden syrup
1 level tsp ground ginger	

- Beat butter to a soft cream, then beat in the caster sugar. They must be very well beaten together.
- Sift the flour, baking powder and the ground ginger, then mix into the creamed mixture.
- Grease the tin and spread the mixture in it. Mark a curved pattern on each slice with a fork.
- Bake in a moderate oven, about gas mark 3 or 350°F, 150°C fan, for about 40 minutes.
- While the shortcake is still hot in the tin, put the ingredients for the icing into a saucepan and melt them together.
- Pour the mixture over the top of the shortcake and spread it evenly.
- Leave the shortcake in the tin and cut into pieces while still warm.
- When cold, ease the slices out with a knife.

Recipe donated by Molly Adams, Souldrop

Jumbo Choc Cookies

3 oz/75g butter
6oz/150g S.R. flour
3oz/75g granulated sugar
pinch salt
3oz/75g soft light brown sugar
2 -4 oz/50 -100g choc chips
Few drops vanilla essence
1 egg (beaten)

- Grease two baking sheets.
- Cream the butter with the sugars and vanilla essence until light and fluffy.
- Beat in the egg.
- Sift flour and salt into the bowl and fold into the creamed mixture.
- Add the choc chips and stir well.
- Drop spoonfuls onto the baking sheets.
- Bake at 180°C/gas mark 4 for 12 -15 minutes.
- Cool on the baking sheets for one minute, and then transfer the cookies to a wire rack to finish cooling.

Recipe donated by Charlie Chamberlayne, Souldrop

Lemon Drizzle Cake

For the cake
4 oz soft butter
6 oz self raising flour
6 oz caster sugar
4 tbsp milk
Grated rind of a large lemon
(unwaxed)
2 eggs

For the syrup
3 tbsp icing sugar
juice of the lemon

- Preheat the oven to 160°C/Gas mark 4.
- Line a 2lb loaf tin or 6 – 7" cake tin, with baking parchment.
- Beat all the cake ingredients together until smooth.
- Scrape the mix into the tin.
- Bake for about an hour, covering the cake after 40 minutes, if it gets too dark.
- Mix the syrup ingredients together.
- While the cake is still warm, prick it all over with a skewer or fork.
- Pour over the syrup.
- Leave it to cool in tin before turning out and serving.

A fabulously simple cake and a favourite of my sweet toothed brother. Also works well baked in muffin cases, only needing about 15 minutes at 200°C/Gas mark 6.

Recipe donated by Caroline Rich, Souldrop

Souldrop Cakes & Biscuits

Milk Chocolate Cake

Cake
7oz Self Raising flour.
8oz caster sugar
½ tsp salt
1oz cocoa
4oz margarine
2 eggs beaten together with
75mls (5 tbsp) evaporated milk
75mls (5tbsp) water
Few drops of vanilla essence

Milk chocolate icing
2 ½ oz margerine
1 x 15mls (1tbsp) cocoa
9oz sieved icing sugar
3 tbsp hot milk
1 tsp vanilla essence

- Sieve flour, sugar, salt, cocoa into a bowl. Rub in margarine.
- Stir in eggs, liquids, vanilla essence. Beat well.
- Grease two 8" round tins. Line with bakewell paper, grease and dust with flour. Divide the mixture between them.
- Bake in moderate oven 170° - 180°c for about 30 minutes.
- When cold sandwich together and cover with milk chocolate icing.
- Chocolate icing – melt margarine in saucepan, blending in cocoa. Stir.
- Add icing sugar, milk and essence.
- Beat until smooth and thick.
- Fill and cover cake. Mark top with a fork.

Recipe donated by Nancy Mills, Souldrop

Mrs Robins' Fruit Cake

4oz margarine
1 level tsp bicarbonate of soda
6oz granulated sugar
1 heaped tsp mixed spice
6oz currants or any mixture of dried fruit
2 beaten eggs

6oz sultanas (I usually put 4oz of each and include dried apricots).
4oz plain flour
2oz chopped peel
4oz self raising flour
1 cup (8oz water)
pinch salt

- Place margarine, sugar, dried fruit, peel, water, bicarbonate of soda and mixed spice in a pan, bring to the boil and simmer for one minute.
- Pour into a large mixing bowl.
- Allow to cool.
- Line a 7 inch square or 8 inch round tin with baking parchment. (I wrap brown paper round the outside and tie it with string).
- Add eggs, flour and salt to the cooled mixture, mix well and pour into tin.
- Bake, centre oven at gas mark 4, 350°F., 180°C for 1 ½ hrs.

Margaret Caiger, in her school days, would make this for her birthday.

Recipe donated by Margaret Caiger, Souldrop

Souldrop Cakes & Biscuits

Muffins

8oz stork
8oz light brown sugar
4 large eggs
12oz of plain flour
2 tsp of baking powder

3 large dsp of cocoa powder
Milk to mix
2 packs of chocolate drops –
white, milk or dark chocolate
Muffin cake tin & muffin cases.

- Pre-heat oven to 180 degrees.
- Put everything into a bowl and mix well (not choc drops) until it drops of the spoon easily.
- Mix in the chocolate drops.
- Once all has been mixed in put large spoonfuls into the muffin case.
- If you fancy grate some choc on top of each one.
- Bake for around 30 minutes or until look golden. They will just start to break open on top when fully cooked… eat WARM…
- You can replace chocolate and cocoa with coconut and cherries and a few drops of vanilla essence OR sultanas and cooking apple cut into small pieces - my favourites).

This recipe is one that has been passed on to me from my late aunt who lost her battle with cancer last year - she was a fabulous cook and worked at school doing the catering. The recipe has been used many times by me and now my son Luke has also mastered the art of perfect muffins. These are meant to be like the big American ones you can buy but with much more taste… and can be varied depending upon taste :)

Recipe donated by Julie Grout, Souldrop

Nanny Caro's
Dinosaur Cookies

4oz softened butter
½ **tsp** bicarbonate of soda
4oz caster sugar
2 tsp ground ginger
9oz plain flour
2 tbsp warmed golden syrup

- Cream the butter and sugar together until very soft.
- Work in the dry ingredients, then the warm runny syrup.
- Mix to a dough.
- Knead well and roll out onto a floured surface.
- Thick cut into shapes of your choice.
- Put the figures onto baking parchment or similar.
- Bake in a moderate oven, 180°c for about 12 minutes or until golden brown.
- Allow to cool slightly before lifting onto a cooling rack.
- Tuck in!

Actually, it is a gingerbread recipe, but my grandchildren have always insisted on cutting it into dinosaur shapes – hence the name. The method is simple enough for children to help, except perhaps the warming and handling of the golden syrup.

Recipe donated by Caroline Rich, Souldrop

Souldrop Cakes & Biscuits

Orange & Lemon Cake

Cake	Orange/lemon butter cream
8oz butter	**6oz** icing sugar
8oz caster sugar	**3oz** butter
4 eggs beaten	Juice of one orange
8oz self-raising flour	or lemon
Grated rind of one orange or lemon	

- Butter two 18cm (7inch) sandwich tins and line the bases with a round of buttered greaseproof paper.
- Beat the butter and sugar together until pale and fluffy. Add the eggs a little at a time, beating well after each addition. Add the finely grated rind of one orange or lemon to the mixture. Fold in half the flour using a metal spoon, then fold in the rest.
- Divide the mixture between the tins and level off with a knife. Bake in the oven at 190 0C (375 0F) for about 20 minutes until they are well risen, firm to the touch and beginning to shrink away from the sides of the tins. Turn out to cool on a wire rack.
- When the cakes are cool, sandwich them together with orange or lemon butter cream. Save a little icing to place on top of the cake.
- To make the butter cream, mix the butter with the icing sugar and the juice of one lemon or orange.

Recipe donated by Janet Fell, Souldrop

Peanut Butter Biscuits

4oz margarine or butter
1 tsp baking powder
4oz caster sugar
1 dsp made coffee
4oz peanut butter
5oz plain flour

- Preheat oven 180°, Gas 4.
- Mix all ingredients together into a paste, shape into a ball.
- Place walnut sized balls onto a greased tray and bake for 20 minutes.

Recipe donated by Jann Horton, Souldrop

Quick & Easy Gingerbread

4oz margarine

8oz plain flour

6oz Demerara sugar

1 tbsp ground ginger

6oz black treacle

2 tbsp milk

4oz golden syrup

½ **level tsp** bicarbonate of soda

2 beaten eggs

- Grease and line a baking tin 9" x 7" (or 8" x 8").
- Cream together margarine and sugar.
- Stir in black treacle and golden syrup.
- Add 2 beaten eggs.
- Stir in flour and ginger.
- Mix milk with bicarbonate of soda and stir in.
- Pour mixture into tin. Sprinkle with chopped stem ginger if you like. Bake 45 – 50 minutes at 170° (until firm in the middle when pressed).
- Leave in tin 10 minutes. Cut into squares.

Nancy's tip – best left one day before eating.

Recipe donated by Nancy Mills, Souldrop

Rock Cakes

8oz Self Raising flour
2oz margarine
¼ tsp salt
6oz dried fruit
½ tsp mixed spice
1 egg
2oz caster sugar
a little milk

- Grease a baking sheet.
- Sift together the flour, salt, mixed spice and sugar.
- Rub in the margarine, and then add the fruit.
- Beat the egg and mix the ingredients with enough milk to make a very stiff mixture.
- Place in about 12 heaps on the baking sheet.
- Sprinkle some sugar over them.
- Bake for 15 – 20 minutes at 190°c.

Try other spices such as cinnamon or nutmeg.

Recipe donated by Robert Freeman, Souldrop

Souldrop Cakes & Biscuits

Shortbread Biscuits

6 oz butter
1oz ground rice
6 oz plain flour
3 oz caster sugar
2 oz cornflour

- Put all ingredients into a mixer and mix thoroughly until mixture forms a ball.
- Roll out, not too thin, onto a lightly floured surface and cut into any shapes you like.
- Bake in oven at 180°C or bottom right oven of an Aga, second shelf down for 10 minutes, or until just turning brown.
- Cut into slices while warm but leave to cool before taking out of tin.

A family favourite from Great Aunt Kathleen.

Recipe donated by the Chamberlaynes, Souldrop

Tree Cake – Baumkuchen

This is a recipe form the north of Germany. It's time consuming but delicious. When cut, the cake reveals the golden rings, like the rings of a tree, giving it its German name, Baumkuchen, which literally means "tree cake".

To get the ring effect, a thin layer of the cake mixture is brushed evenly onto a baking tin and baked until golden. Then another layer of cake mixture is added and baked. And another...

Traditionally the town of Salzwedel and the Master Baker for the Prussian King have been associated with its creation in 1790.

200g butter	**80g** flour
100g marzipan	**70g** cornflour
100g sugar	**1 tsp** lemon zest
1 pinch of salt	**5** egg whites
1 tbsp vanilla sugar (or **1 tsp** vanilla extract)	**1** pinch of salt
	100g sugar
5 egg yolks	**100-150g** plain dark chocolate

- Prepare your cake tin. Butter the base and the sides of the tin and then line the base with baking paper.
- Preheat oven to 220°C.
- Have all the ingredients at room temperature. Mix butter with the marzipan, salt and the sugar. If the marzipan isn't soft enough warm it carefully (just a few seconds!) in the microwave to soften it – if it's too hard it won't mix with the other ingredients properly.
- Add the egg yolks and mix.
- Add the flour and the cornflour to the mixture.
- Whisk the egg whites with the salt until nearly stiff.
- Slowly add sugar until you have a glossy stiff mixture.
- Carefully fold the egg white mixture into butter mix.
- Now spread the first (very thin!) layer into the base of your tin and bake in oven for about 3 to 4 minutes or until dough is browned.
- Take the tin out of the oven and spread the next thin layer and put it under the grill. Continue to bake layer after layer until the dough is finished. Watch each layer very carefully as it will burn very quickly if left too long!
- Let the cake cool in the tin. Remove cake form the tin.
- Melt the chocolate either in the microwave (with short 25 second boosts) or in a water bath and spread evenly on the cake.

Recipe donated by Angela & Christof Schloesser, Souldrop

Old Church Farm, October 2009.

The Old Church Farm.

George and Mildred, residents of Charm Cottage and not for the table.

Two white doves – live with other doves and bats, bringing peace and harmony to Souldrop. July 2009.

George, dressed up in his Sunday best – pet kune kune pig, residing at Charm Cottage.

All Saints Church, Souldrop, October 2009.

Souldrop Sauces

Salad Cream

2 dsp of condensed milk
1tsp mustard
Salt & pepper
Milk to mix
Vinegar

- Mix condensed milk with mustard, salt and pepper.
- Cream with milk.
- Add vinegar to thin to the right consistency.

This was my late father's recipe that I always enjoyed as a child. It is lovely as an addition to most sandwiches, especially with salad in them. I often find sandwiches a bit boring, and this recipe really adds a kick to them. It is great with any meal that is accompanied with a side salad eg barbeques, quiches etc. I am not sure if Sean actually liked this, as he was very fussy, but he had a very close relationship with my Dad, who I inherited the recipe from.

Recipe donated by Kay Bone, Souldrop (Sean's Mum)

Smokey BBQ Sauce

1 oz butter
1 onion, chopped and peeled
1 clove garlic crushed
2 tbsp white wine vinegar
1/4 pint water
1 tbsp English mustard
2 tbsp demerara sugar

1 slice lemon
1 bay leaf
Pinch cayenne pepper
1 tbsp Worcester sauce
6 tbsp tomato ketchup
2 tbsp tomato puree
salt and pepper

- Melt butter, add onion and garlic and fry till soft but NOT brown.
- Then add: white wine vinegar, water, English mustard, demerara sugar, lemon, bay leaf, cayenne pepper.
- Bring all this to the boil then simmer for 15 minutes.
- Then add: Worcester sauce, tomato ketchup, tomato puree, salt and pepper.
- Then simmer for a further 5 - 10 minutes.

This is really delicious. Store it in a plastic container in the freezer for up to two months.

Recipe donated by Charlie Butler-Henderson & Zoe Fryer, Souldrop

Apple & Blackberry Jam

12oz (375g) apples (after peeling and coring)
2 1b (1kg) blackberries
¼ pt (150 mls) water
3 1b (1.5 kg) granulated sugar
½ oz (15g) butter

- Slice the apples thinly and put into a large saucepan with blackberries and water.
- Bring to the boil, reduce the heat and simmer in a covered pan for 10-15 minutes.
- Crush the fruit against the sides of the pan until soft and pulpy.
- Add the sugar, heat slowly, stirring continuously until the sugar dissolves.
- Bring to the boil and boil briskly for 10-15 minutes (or until setting point is reached).
- Remove from the heat and stir in the butter to disperse scum.
- Pour into pots and cover while hot. Makes 5lb (2.5kg) jam.

*Hedgerow blackberries and crab apples make the best jam but discard any mouldy blackberries. Crab apples provide a tarter flavour than dessert apples.

Recipe donated by Janet Fell, Souldrop

Corn Bread

75g cornmeal
200mls milk
100g plain flour
1 egg well beaten
3 tsp baking powder
2 tbsp shortening (butter, chicken fat or beef dripping)
30g sugar
¾ tsp salt

- Sift and mix dry ingredients.
- Add milk, egg and shortening.
- Bake in a shallow buttered baking tin (8" x 8")
  for 20 minutes at 220°c - 200° fan oven.

Recipe donated by Robert Freeman, Souldrop

Souldrop Miscellaneous

Easy Chocolate Truffles

(With thanks to James Martin!)

> **200g/7oz** dark chocolate, broken into pieces
> **175mls/6fl oz** double cream
> **5 tbsp** brandy, rum or other spirit of your choice (optional)
> cocoa, icing sugar or finely crushed nuts, to finish

- Cover a baking tray tightly with two layers of cling film to put the truffles on to set.
- Tip the chocolate pieces into a bowl.
- Pour the cream into a pan and bring to a rolling boil.
- Pour over the chocolate and stir until all the chocolate is melted. If you want to add booze, mix it in at this point.
- Allow the mixture to cool at room temperature - this will take about 1½ hours - by which time it should be set.
- Using a melon baller or teaspoon, scoop out bite-sized pieces. Dust your hands with icing sugar to stop them sticking and roll the pieces into balls.
- Roll in sifted icing sugar, cocoa or crushed nuts and place them on the prepared tray.
- Once they are set you can store them in an airtight container in the fridge for about a week.
  Makes approximately 15 individual truffles.

Recipe donated by Jon and Beckie Smith, Souldrop

A Tip From Jo Fletcher, Mayfield, Souldrop

Buy concentrated frozen orange juice - Waitrose sells it. It has to be frozen as that has a stronger flavour. Add about 2 scoops or tablespoons to:

- Gravy
- Cream
- Mashed potatoes
- Stock
- Fantastic with chicken
- Any recipe that doesn't normally have a kick.

Toffee popcorn

2 oz popcorn	**1 tbsp** golden syrup
1 oz melted margarine or butter	**½ oz** butter or margarine
Toffee	**1 tbsp** water
2oz brown sugar	**1 tbsp** vinegar

- Heat butter and popcorn over a high heat in a large saucepan, shaking until "pops" stop.
- Boil all the toffee ingredients for three minutes without stirring, then pour over the popped corn quickly and stir in.

Recipe donated by Jann Horton, Souldrop

By hook or by crook,
I will be last in this book!

Sean washing up to the amusement of his mother at his housewarming, when he cooked for family and friends in his flat in Olney, May 2008.